UNIVERSITY OF NORTH CAROLINA AT CHAPEL HILL
DEPARTMENT OF ROMANCE LANGUAGES

NORTH CAROLINA STUDIES
IN THE ROMANCE LANGUAGES AND LITERATURES

Founder: URBAN TIGNER HOLMES

Distributed by:

UNIVERSITY OF NORTH CAROLINA PRESS
CHAPEL HILL
North Carolina 27514
U.S.A.

NORTH CAROLINA STUDIES IN THE
ROMANCE LANGUAGES AND LITERATURES

Number 214

THE FICTIONS OF THE SELF
THE EARLY WORKS OF MAURICE BARRÈS

THE FICTIONS OF THE SELF
THE EARLY WORKS OF MAURICE BARRÈS

BY

GORDON SHENTON

CHAPEL HILL

NORTH CAROLINA STUDIES IN THE ROMANCE
LANGUAGES AND LITERATURES

U.N.C. DEPARTMENT OF ROMANCE LANGUAGES

1979

Library of Congress Cataloging in Publication Data

Shenton, Gordon.
  The fictions of the self.

  (North Carolina studies in the Romance languages and literatures; no. 214)
  Bibliography: p.
  1. Barrès, Maurice, 1862-1923 — Criticism and interpretation. I. Title. II. Series.

PQ2603.A52Z877   843'.0'12   79-21065
ISBN 0-8078-9214-9

I. S. B. N. 0-8078-9214-9

DEPÓSITO LEGAL: V. 2.282-1979   I. S. B. N. 84-499-3076-6
ARTES GRÁFICAS SOLER, S. A. - JÁVEA, 28 - VALENCIA (8) - 1979

ACKNOWLEDGMENTS

I wish to express my thanks to Professor W. M. Frohock of Harvard University for his constant support and to the Camargo Foundation in Cassis for the grant which enabled me to work on this book in such pleasant circumstances.

CONTENTS

	Page
INTRODUCTION	11
CHAPTER	
I. SETTING OUT IN LIFE	21
II. THE CONQUEST OF ENERGY	42
1. Sensibility	42
2. The Self and the World	51
3. The Cult of the Self	56
4. Liberty and Identity	66
III. THE BODY	74
IV. THE ALLEGORIES OF THE SELF	96
V. THE ANALOGICAL UNIVERSE	117
CONCLUSION	142
BIBLIOGRAPHY	155

INTRODUCTION

The Barresian legacy is essentially a certain attitude and a certain stance in relation to life and literature, which were to have a profound influence upon the way the following generation conceived the literary vocation. It lies in his characteristic conception of the function of literature itself and in the use to which he put it. The idea which lies at the heart of his activity as a man of letters is that his own life, his own spiritual destiny in the world, is a work to be fashioned and created, and that the role of literature is to be at the same time the means and the locus of this creation. His principal subject is the spiritual confrontation of the individual self with the world, which appears both as a "vast spectacle" and a field of action in the enterprise of self-discovery and self-creation.

My purpose is to study the dynamics of this self-creation in the first group of texts which Barrès wrote: the allegorical novels and stories of his youth. This series of works, which form an organic group by the continuity of their themes and techniques, begins with the *Nouvelle pour les rêveurs,* published in the first number of *Les Taches d'encre,* and includes the three novels of *Le Culte du moi (Sous l'œil des barbares, Un Homme libre,* and *Le Jardin de Bérénice), L'Ennemi des lois,* and the short story, *Un Amateur d'âmes,* which opens *Du sang, de la volupté et de la mort.*[1] After *Du sang,* his work took a different direction with

---

[1] The four numbers of *Les Taches d'encre (Gazette mensuelle par M. Maurice Barrès)* appeared between November 1884 and February 1885. *Sous l'œil des barbares* was published at the end of November, 1887, *Un Homme libre* in 1889, *Le Jardin de Bérénice* in 1891, *L'Ennemi des lois* in 1892, and *Du sang, de la volupté et de la mort* in 1894.

the publication of *Les Déracinés* in 1897. The early works were concerned uniquely with his own spiritual development and his personal adaptation to the outside world. The political question was raised in both *Le Jardin de Bérénice* and *L'Ennemi des lois*, but it involved the spiritual and moral preconditions of personal political commitment. *Le Roman de l'énergie nationale (Les Déracinés, Leurs Figures,* and *L'Appel au soldat)* and *Les Bastions de l'Est (Au service de l'Allemagne, Colette Baudoche,* and *Le Génie du Rhin)* expand the themes which he developed around the problems of the solitary egotist to the dimension of the collective life of the nation. One of the objectives of my analysis is to show that the works which were written after 1897, when the Dreyfus affair gave such impetus to his "nationalist" themes, are an extension of the early works not only in terms of ideas and themes but also in terms of techniques, textual organization, and fictional schemas. The triangular structure, illustrated in *Le Jardin de Bérénice* by the trio Philippe, Bérénice, and the Adversary (or the Barbarian), underlies much of his work. It is this structure which enables him to generate the different texts in which the themes of his sensibility and its confrontation with the world are articulated and set in motion.

This study, then, has two aspects. First of all, it is an analysis of a literary sensibility, which I shall try to describe in terms of its themes and of a certain number of dynamic tensions: between life and literature; between the deadening influence of the previous generation of writers and thinkers and the aspirations of the young generation for which Barrès was the self-conscious champion; between the morbid tendencies of Decadence and the desire for spiritual renewal which was so characteristic of the late 19th Century; between the cult of personal perfection and the collective ideal of nationalism; between the idea of self-creation

---

In references within my text to the works most frequently quoted, the following abbreviations will be used:

Sous l'œil des barbares: SB
Un Homme libre: HL
Le Jardin de Bérénice: JB
L'Ennemi des lois: EL
Du sang, de la volupté et de la mort: SVM

Except where otherwise indicated, all references are to the definitive edition established by the Librairie Plon.

as action, commitment, and even fanaticism and the idea of self-creation as an inner harmony based on understanding and acceptance. His project is to explore the problem of life, to elucidate the confrontation of the Self and the world in both its individual and its social dimensions, and ultimately to create within the space of the text a complex equilibrium of the conflicting tendencies inside him.

The second major objective of my study, which I shall conduct parallel to the first, is to describe the literary forms engendered by Barrès. I shall attempt to isolate certain basic structures which recur throughout his writing: the organization of his works around moments of intense meditative experience and the way these meditations lead to the composition of the text at many levels; the dialectical structure of the novels and of Barrès' later political thought in which the individual or the nation strive to affirm their consciousness under the menace of some adversary principle; the use of allegory and the use of history in such a way that the outside world is reduced to the categories of the Self while providing a system of signs or lessons to guide the egotist in his development.

* * *

Barrès is chiefly remembered as a moralist — that is, his influence has been in the sphere of values, ideas, and ways of feeling — and he is not usually associated with innovation in the practice of the novel. In fact many readers consider him to be only marginally a novelist, given the large proportion of non-fiction within his work and the very "unfictional" nature of many of his novels. However, it must be emphasized that, when Barrès' work, particularly his early work, is placed within the context of the late 80s and the 90s, it can be seen to have played an important role in a fundamental transformation of the novel which took place in those years. In a complete reversal, the objective, "scientific", third person fictional illusions of the naturalist school were displaced by self-centered, often first person novels. The books of Huysmans, Barrès, Gide, and Proust, who were the most important architects of this transformation introduced not only new subject matter and new techniques, but a new conception of the function of the novel.

Its scope was significantly widened beyond the creation of realist illusions of life to include new areas of psychological investigation within the direct personal experience of the novelist. As a vehicle of introspection, the novel became increasingly involved with attitudes to life and with the working out of such subjective problems as identity and authenticity of being. As a vehicle of involvement with the outside world, it took up a variety of religious, philosophical, psychological, and even political concerns. A strong didactic element made itself apparent in the preoccupation with values, in the use of literature as a therapeutic measure, and in the new type of relationship which was established between the writer and his reader. Barrès and Gide both had a marked pedagogical bent, and sought to draw the reader into their own moral enquiries.

For Barrès, the novel was not a means of telling stories, inventing characters, describing setting and social *milieu,* and imagining a significant action. He was not concerned with acquiring knowledge about the outside world. Fiction for him is a projection of his inner life, an articulation of his sense of himself at the deepest level where intellectual reflexion merges with the shifting certainties and uncertainties of the Self. It is a means of self-discovery because it is integrated into the ongoing process of questioning and search which makes up the dynamism of life, especially in youth. In *Sous l'oeil des Barbares,* he uses a fairly conventional allegorical technique to project the reality of his soul. In the later chapters of this same novel and in *Un Homme libre* where he switches to the first person narrative, he fictionalizes the inner life of his character through the device of the spiritual journal. *Le Jardin de Bérénice,* by far the most technically sophisticated of the trilogy, weaves an allegorical tapestry out of the splendid desolation of Aigues-Mortes. But in all cases, the fictional representation of himself as the young man, later called Philippe, allows Barrès to project the themes of his spiritual life in an "ideal" form — that is, as ideas having a concrete existence within the world of the novel. Indeed, he called these works Ideological Novels.

Within them, he can not only give shape and reality to the inconsistent gropings of consciousness, but by a process of amplification and hyperbole he is able to construct his own unity and to forge a characteristic stance. Philippe's elaboration of a psychological technique for detaching himself from the existential downpull of life and rising above the world in a state of self-induced fervor in *Un Homme libre* cannot be read as just an autobiographical transposition of Barrès' own experience. The book makes the experience and creates the attitudes; it is in this sense that Barrès, the public figure and the moral guide, is the creation of his writing.

So the fictional process for Barrès is not the invention of story, but the creation of relationships among his thoughts and feelings at a certain distance from himself. At the heart of his endeavor is his search for a voice and a manner which would allow him to situate his self-creation in a realm quite different from that of life. The "literariness" of the novel, its supposed removal from real experience, and its assumption of closure and completion are essential to this process. Within the novel, everything is fiction in the sense that I have tried to define, not just the more obviously novelistic aspects of *Le Culte du moi* but even, at the other extreme, the critical passages on Sainte-Beuve and Constant and the treatise on Lorraine in *Un Homme libre*. The "Universe"[2] is the central image used by Barrès in his early work to denote this literary space in which states of mind, emotions, reflections on many topics, real historical events, personnages and anecdotes

---

[2] *L'univers* is one of those words which occur very frequently in Barrès' works to constitute a special, idiosyncratic vocabulary. Sometimes he uses the word to mean the outside world as it is perceived by the egotist: "L'univers me pénètre et se développe et s'harmonise en moi" (SB. p. 245). Very often, it signifies the egotist's inner world, the mental reality of his thoughts, ideals, and sentiments. In this sense, it is the world as it appears in the mirror of his mind. "Dans un univers qui n'est que l'ensemble de ses pensées régnera la belle ordonnance selon laquelle s'adaptent nécessairement les unes aux autres les conceptions d'un cerveau lucide" (*Examen des trois romans idéologiques* in the Plon edition of *Sous l'œil des barbares*, p. 33).

However, outside and inside are really identical since reality is only appearance: "C'est nous qui créons l'univers" (*Examen*, p. 32). Thus it comes to mean the ideal creation which is the objective of his egotism. It is a perfected vision of the world in which the individual harmonizes outside reality with his own subjectivity. In *L'Examen*, for instance, he writes: "L'univers n'est qu'une fresque qu'il [le Moi] fait belle ou laide" (p. 39). The image of the fresco conveys the deliberate and artificial nature of this creation.

coexist with invented characters and situations in the "fictional" harmony of style and form. The carry-over of the techniques which he evolved in his early works to later books which are not presented as novels is an indication of the extent to which writing in general became a question of transforming subjectivity into "ideological" fictions.

It was Symbolism that gave the first impetus to the inward direction which the novel was to take. It opposed its solipsistic pessimism to the social vision of naturalist pessimism, denying any reality to the outside world and affirming the solitude of the individual within the confines of his own consciousness. J.-K. Huysmans' *A rebours*, although it remains within the general framework of the naturalist manner (third person narrative, a story presented as a psycho-physiological case study, extensive documentation), reduces the objective world to the villa in which Des Esseintes encloses himself. And, in fact, this suburban refuge is clearly a figure of the inner space of his mind, the world of his esthetic tastes, his memories, and his fantasies. Paul Bourget, in his influential essay upon Baudelaire in the *Essais de psychologie contemporaine* describes very succinctly the artistic orientation which had become so widespread and of which Huysmans' book is such a striking illustration. "Si les citoyens d'une décadence sont inférieurs comme ouvriers de la grandeur du pays, ne sont-ils pas très supérieurs comme artistes de l'intérieur de leur âme?"[3] We are very close to the sources of Barrès' initial inspiration here. Philippe's ambition in *Le Culte du moi* to be the artist of his own soul is expressly rooted in the conviction that the Self is the only reality and that the outside world ("si néfaste" [HL p. 39]) has no objective validity. The metaphor of the *univers* is an expression of this solipsistic vision of the world as it appears to the individual, not the outside world itself, but the mental image of it, the reconstruction of reality within the space of the mind.

Since the world is nothing more than appearance and ways of seeing things, the egotist is free, by an effort of revolt and creative will, to remodel the world in his own image. A remarkable text, written in early 1886, reveals that this idea, so central to the

---

[3] Paul Bourget, *Essais de psychologie contemporaine*, Paris, Lemerre, 1883, p. 27.

development of Barrès' work, was in his mind well before he conceived *Le Culte du moi* and that it has its roots in the subjective idealism out of which the Symbolist esthetic was being elaborated. In "L'Esthétique de demain: L'Art suggestif" which he published in *De Nieuwe Gids* of January, 1886, he was reflecting on Teodor de Wyzewa's article on the "Pessimisme de Wagner."

> En quelques pages profondes de *la Revue wagnérienne* M. Teodor de Wyzewa formule l'état d'âme qui réalisera *l'Art suggestif* de demain.
> L'appellation Pessimisme succède désormais à Romantisme, Réalisme, Naturalisme. Être plus pessimistes que les romantiques ou les naturalistes, les nouveaux venus ne le pourraient pas, seulement ils le sont d'une autre façon. — L'univers où nous vivons est un rêve. Il n'y a point de choses, point d'hommes, ou plutôt il y a tout cela, mais parce que l'Être se doit nécessairement projeter en des apparences; et notre douleur aussi est le volontaire effet de notre âme; nous projetons au Néant extérieur l'image de notre essence intime, puis croyant à l'existence de cet univers qui n'est que le reflet de notre Moi, nous souffrons de ses incohérences, notre simple ouvrage cependant. — Mais sous l'influence d'idées nouvelles nous avons pénétré ce cauchemar, nous nous sommes connus seules causes de cette incohérence, de cette diversité des intérêts et des choses, de cette angoisse: nous renonçons à l'égoïsme. Puisque tout l'univers est nous-mêmes, nous l'aimerons, nous nous y mêlons; par la compassion sur le Monde, c'est-à-dire sur nous-mêmes, nous ferons l'unité qui supprime la souffrance du Moi, se débattant contre l'extérieur. — Cependant le sage fera plus encore, il renoncera à ce monde connu, aux apparences actuelles qui l'entourent, même après les avoir revêtues de l'unité par la compassion. Et puisque rien des hommes, des choses, du monde enfin n'existe que par lui, il changera son mode de créer, et au-dessus de l'univers présent il bâtira un univers nouveau; et jouissant sans limite, il sera l'artiste, l'extraordinaire ménétrier qui retient et gouverne la danse idéale des choses. [4]

---

[4] Quoted by Marie-Thérèse Goosse in "A propos de *Sous l'œil des barbares*," *La Revue d'histoire littéraire de la France*, LXVI (1966), 672.

The principal themes of the trilogy are already contained in this text: the desire to transcend the painful separation of the Self and the world in an exaltation of consciousness, the search for the unity of the Self in harmony with its world, the extension of self-love to universal compassion, and the urge to omnipotence. But Barrès' thought can be seen to be taking a direction quite different from that taken by Symbolism. He does not propose a flight out of the world or the substitution of this world by a dream construction. On the contrary, by a strange reversal, he draws closer to the outside world; he will find the spiritual strength to accept it again and to become involved in it ("nous l'aimerons, nous nous y mêlons"). And better still, he will invent a method to divert artistic creativity (which Symbolism opposes to reality) back towards the reality of the world. His premises are the same as those of Symbolism — the world is a dream, material reality is a source of suffering — but by carrying Schopenhaurian pessimism[5] to its extreme point of total negation, he will achieve a liberation of the mind from the weight of despair. He will seek to transform the inertia of nihilism into renewed energy and enthusiasm.

Barrès' project is to harness the energy of an initial movement of revolt in an effort to discover authentic points of contact between the Self and the world. Egotism is at once a quest and a construction. He is striving first of all to make the outside world conform to his own being by negating everything that is alien in it and by reducing it to a new ideological space in which he

---

[5] Schopenhauer's thought was introduced into France in 1870 by Challemel-Lacour in his article "Un Bouddhiste contemporain en Allemagne, Arthur Schopenhauer," *Revue des deux mondes* (March 15, 1870), pp. 296-332. See M.-C. Bancquart, *Les Écrivains et l'histoire*, p. 18.

In his critical writings, Barrès often referred to the current of nihilism in French literature. He had studied Leconte de Lisle as an example of the "modern disenchantment" (*Les Taches d'encre*, reprinted in *L'Œuvre de Maurice Barrès*, "Au club de l'Honnête Homme," I, 456) so characteristic of an age of intellectual disarray. He had even planned a series of essays on "Le Nihilisme contemporain" for *Les Taches d'encre* (Ida-Marie Frandon, *L'Orient de Maurice Barrès. Étude de genèse*, Geneva, Droz and Lille, Giard, 1952, p. 42 and note 34). Mme Frandon discusses at length Barrès' concern with the question of nihilism when he was a young man. For her, it is one of the first acquisitions of that "Culture d'Orient" which is the subject of Chapter III of her thesis.

can control all the elements. Self-possession and possession of the world are to be acquired simultaneously in the reconstructed "universe". When this assimilation, or interiorization, has neutralized the dangerous otherness of the world, the egotist is ready to seek a creative involvement in life. The last phase of this dialectic between the Self and the World is an outward movement back towards identification with something outside the individual.

Of course, this rearrangement of the world into a meaningful harmony is only possible in the space of the literary text. Philippe pursues in the fictional "reality" of Barrès' novels what Barrès sought to achieve in writing. So Philippe is not simply a thinly disguised Barrès, a direct transfer of the voice that says "I", but an allegorical representation of his creator's literary self in its confrontation with his own mental universe. The "universe" is, then, the ideological space of writing in which Barrès seeks to harmonize the new being within himself with the world which he has ordered to reflect his idea. The transposition of reality into literature is accomplished by a complex process of interiorization, reduction, and reconstruction.

Chapter I

SETTING OUT IN LIFE

When Barrès arrived in Paris in 1882, he was equipped with a conquering ambition and a firm sense of his literary vocation, but very little else. He had no idea of what his subject should be, nor, *a fortiori,* of what genre and form he should adopt. He began with articles of literary criticism in which he sought to assimilate and define for himself the state of modern literature: pieces on Victor Hugo, Auguste Vacquerie, Anatole France, Maurice Rollinat, Baudelaire, and Leconte de Lisle. These earliest critical essays in the *Journal de la Meurthe et des Vosges, La Jeune France,* and then in his own *Les Taches d'encre* already reveal his dominant interest in general problems of individual and collective psychology. The title of his article on Baudelaire in the first number of *Les Taches d'encre* is indicative of the turn his critical interest was taking: "Psychologie contemporaine (La sensation en littérature). La Folie de Charles Baudelaire." The first part of the title is a clear allusion to Bourget's *Essais de psychologie contemporaine.* The study of Leconte de Lisle in the third number is called "Psychologie: Une nouvelle manière de sentir," a title which announces his abiding preoccupation with ways of feeling. "Psychology," as he uses the word, means little more than this.

Until he came upon the formula for *Sous l'œil des Barbares,* it was difficult to imagine a way to turn his analytic passion for ideas and problems of sensibility into the material for a novel. He wrote a few short stories for *Les Taches d'encre* in which one can see in embryonic form many of the themes and techniques of his novels, but he himself did not at first envisage writing a novel at all. He planned originally to publish a collection of these stories under the title *Le Départ pour la vie*.[1]

He was not attracted to the straightforward realist or naturalist novel, either by taste or by talent. In November, 1882, for instance, we find him writing to Léon Sorg that he was going to set himself a program of reading "pour sortir des sempiternels romans."[2] Clearly, he was not interested in adding another "objective" study of contemporary *mores* to the list. Moreover, his imagination was not naturally inclined to the creation of fictions of this sort. He was never really at home with the manipulation of three-dimensional characters, convincing plots, or well described *milieux*, even in *Les Déracinés* in which, for once, he adopted the naturalist mode.

However, Barrès began writing in a decade in which dissatisfaction with the naturalist formula was generalized and which saw the emergence of what Michel Raimond has called "the crisis of the novel."[3] Undoubtedly, he benefited from the esthetic anarchy of the situation which made it possible to call just about anything a novel. A multitude of innovations and theories appeared in reaction to a conception of the novel which had dominated the literary scene for so long that its possibilities seemed to have been exhausted. The growing opposition to naturalism surfaced in 1887 with the *Manifeste des cinq* against Zola after the publication of *La Terre*. The prestige of naturalism was shaken in these years by a succession of blows: the defection of Huysmans, the Symbolist attacks on the naturalist vision of the world, the anti-naturalist declarations of many writers in Jules Huret's *Enquête sur l'évolution littéraire* in 1891.

---

[1] *Le Départ pour la vie*, Paris, Plon, 1961, p. 212. The title which Barrès proposed to give his collection of *nouvelles* has been most appropriately taken up by the publishers of this volume of correspondance written during the years of his literary *début*. See also, M.-T. Goosse, "A propos de *Sous l'œil des barbares*," p. 657.

[2] Letter dated November 21, 1882. *Le Départ pour la vie*, p. 132. As early as 1880, he proclaimed his distaste for the "commun vulgaire des romanciers" with the one exception of Balzac (letter to Léon Sorg of October 10, 1880, *Le Départ pour la vie*, p. 46).

[3] Michel Raimond, *La Crise du roman des lendemains du naturalisme aux années vingt*, Paris, Corti, 1967.

In reaction to naturalism and under the impetus of Symbolism, Barrès and others took the novel in an inward direction, placing the problems of the individual consciousness at the center of attention. As I have noted, Huysmans' *A rebours* in 1884 was a turning point in this autobiographical reorientation of the genre. There appeared a large number of more or less fanciful heroes who were projections of their creator's intellectual experience: Huysmans' Des Esseintes and Durtal; Jules Vallès' Jacques Vingtras; Barrès' Philippe; Rémy de Gourmont's Hubert d'Entragues in *Sixtine*; Anatole France's Sylvestre Bonnard, Jérôme Coignard and Monsieur Bergeret; and Pierre Loti, at once hero and author. A concurrent development was that the novel became a catch-all for the expression of all kinds of personal ideas. Often, the novel form appeared little more than a convenient structuring device for material that was certainly not fictional in nature.[4] *A rebours* is at once a collection of critical essays, a catalogue of curiosities, an anthology of prose poems, and a treatise on various recondite arts. Taken as a whole, it is a psychological study, an "analytic" novel. As fiction, there is little one can say about it. The novels of Huysmans, Barrès, Bloy, France, and many others are examples of what Northrop Frye calls the anatomical novel.[5] That is to say, they are more concerned with the dissection of philosophical, psychological, and moral problems than with creating fictional illusions. *Le Culte du moi*, which brings a combination of philosophy, psychology, religion, and lyricism to bear on the problems of the individual seeking to find his way in a difficult world, was perfectly attuned to the taste of the late eighties.

The times were very propitious, then, for the kind of novel that Barrès was able to write and *Le Culte du moi* was successful on two levels. It preached a creative defense of the Self at a time of intellectual and moral crisis and it provided a highly original example of a novel which takes place almost entirely in the mind of its hero and in which plot and action are reduced to the movements of his psychic states. Ideas and feelings, dra-

---

[4] Michel Raimond speaks of "une crise de l'affabulation" at the end of the century (*La Crise du roman*, p. 55).

[5] Northrop Frye, *The Anatomy of Criticism: Four Essays*, Princeton, Princeton University Press, 1957.

matized in various ways, constitute the substance of these novels, so that Barrès was able to dispense with the naturalist formula altogether. Indeed, *Le Culte du moi* was one of the most radically anti-naturalist works of the late nineteenth century, more so certainly than the works of Huysmans or Anatole France.

The genesis of *Sous l'œil des Barbares,* and hence of *Le Culte du moi* in general, is very revealing. Particularly in the case of the first two novels in the trilogy, Barrès' problem was to find an overall fictional structure which would allow him to weld together the different kinds of material he had ready: short allegorical fictions, anecdotes based on significant moments in his intellectual development, and reflections on diverse subjects in essay form. Barrès came to the novel by way of the short story, which was enjoying a considerable vogue in the Symbolist period, precisely because of the scorn in which many writers held the ponderous machinery of the novel.[6]

As Mme Goosse has pointed out in her important article on the genesis of *Sous l'œil des barbares,*[7] it is *Nouvelle pour les rêveurs* (Barrès' earliest piece of fiction, published in the first number of *Les Taches d'encre*)[8] which is the starting point for his first novel. Specifically the story provides the material for Chapter One of *Sous l'œil des barbares,* "Départ inquiet," although in a considerably altered form.[9] The "Bonhomme Système" and M. X... are clearly derived from the figure of Monsieur de Rougemont, and the young man is in the same position as Daniel Camille between the teachings of philosophy and the example of a young woman's unintellectual sensibility. Barrès eliminates all the naturalist elements of *Nouvelle pour les rêveurs.* The characters no longer have names and the setting is a vague sensualist never-never land, a symbolist paradise of languor and glowing beauty. The meaning of the philosophical allegory is much more ambiguous and the element of satire directed against the Master — already discretely present in the short story — is much more discernable.

---

[6] *La Crise du roman,* p. 65.
[7] "A propos de *Sous l'œil des barbares,*" *Revue d'histoire littéraire de la France,* LXVI (1966).
[8] *Nouvelle pour les rêveurs* in *Les Taches d'encre,* No. I (November 5, 1884), reprinted in *L'Œuvre de Maurice Barrès,* I, 410.
[9] Mme Goosse, "A propos de *Sous l'œil des barbares,*" pp. 659-662.

Nouvelle pour les rêveurs provides more than just the basis for the first chapter, however. It is the starting point of the whole novel in as much as the connecting thread in an otherwise disjointed book is the young man's quest among various possible attitudes for a way of adapting to the problems of existence. The young woman undergoes various transformations and several philosophical, ethical, and intellectual positions are portrayed in the novel, but the formula remains the same. The title of the novel is given by another of the stories from *Les Taches d'encre,* this time from the last number in early 1885. *Héroïsmes superflus* becomes Chapter Three, "Désintéressement," in which we find the Barbarians threatening the noble Ideal. This is an end-of-empire philosophical allegory in which declining paganism clashes with rising Christianity, decadent civilization with vital barbarism.

Sous l'œil des barbares is manifestly a patchwork of unrelated fragments. It is in no sense a continuous novel. Barrès presents the chapters as *tableaux* which evoke in an indirect and suggestive manner the "six or seven different realities" (SB, p. 51) of the young man's mental universe. As Mme Goosse shows,[10] the novel was the compilation of a number of disparate texts linked only by their thematic similarity. Each chapter has an independent history and the early ones were written before the project to unite them in a single volume was clearly conceived. What caused Barrès to abandon his original project to publish a book of *nouvelles* under the title *Le Départ pour la vie* and to work instead on *Sous l'œil des barbares* was, I think, the possibility he foresaw of establishing a thematic coherence around the subject of the young man's quest for a formula for living. "Setting out in life" was Barrès' great subject in the early years, from its beginnings in *Nouvelle pour les rêveurs* to *Les Déracinés* where the same theme is treated in a different mode.

This early work exploits two areas of experience, both directly related to his own life: the disarray faced by a sensitive boy as

---

[10] The composition of what now constitutes *Sous l'œil des barbares* covers the years 1883-87 (Mme Goosse, "A propos de *Sous l'œil des barbares,*" p. 669). The first half of the book is made up of material from the days of *Les Taches d'encre* and two of the three chapters in this part were published independently.

he grows up in the French school system and the ambition of the aspiring young writer and politician in the capital. To a large extent, *Le Culte du moi* dramatizes a situation which was shared by almost all sensitive *bacheliers* as they stood on the threshold of their lives: [11] frustration, intellectual yearning, and a bookish desire for a higher form of spiritual fulfillment. The theme of ambition is perhaps less obvious than that of intellectual revolt, but it underlies many of the developments in *Le Culte du moi* and it reappears more openly in *Les Déracinés*. Philippe is, of course, no realist hero bent on material success, but his quest is for a stance in life which would put him among the spiritual elite. He is constantly measuring himself against others even when he is most contemptuously debunking the whole intellectual and moral tradition of the century. From the beginning, then, his work combines a strong negative reaction and a forward-looking, questing movement towards something new and spiritually satisfying. It is turned against the whole educational, cultural, and political establishment and it seeks to find new ground for the erection of an original ethic.

Barrès is usually seen today as a conservative writer, and there is perhaps a tendency to read the works of his youth in the light of his own later attitudes and also in the light of attitudes which were formed about him many years afterwards, so that much of the freshness and impact of these books is lost. His reputation as a champion of traditional values obscures the fact that as a young man he, too, was a dissident in the long tradition of 19th century rebels against the established moral and literary order. His early books, and indeed the whole edifice of his work, are marked by a revolt which is at once political, literary, and spiritual in its thrust. However, the terms of reference in the period of French intellectual history after 1870 are quite different from

---

[11] See Justin O'Brien, *The Novel of Adolescence in France*, for a discussion of the theme of childhood in Barrès' works. O'Brien underlines the originality of his decision to write about and for adolescents, staking his reputation on the acclaim of schoolboys: "If one asks why he took this risk, the only answer is that, his extremely sensitive nature having been most strongly marked by his adolescent sufferings, he recognized what adolescents needed and felt he could supply it. Thus he wrote as an older brother, hardly out of school, whose experiences in finding himself might serve as a model for his *cadets*" (p. 73).

the values of revolt in more recent times. In cultural circles, opposition to the young Third Republic was most vociferous on the right. Nevertheless Barrès' "reactionary" attack upon democratic institutions and certain orthodoxes of thought in Republican France was, in the context of his age, a modern, non-conformist stance.

He was idolized by the younger generation of the 1880s and 90s because of the spirit of arrogant disrespect and independence which pervades his writings. *Le Culte du moi* begins as a thoroughgoing rejection of everything that the world has to offer a young man. It denounces the moral and philosophical bankruptcy of the age and the emptiness of all the formulas for success which are available to the young generation as they set out in life. In the political sphere, his literary debut in 1888 with *Sous l'œil des barbares* was closely connected to the agitation around the figure of General Boulanger whose cause he championed against the "two thousand mediocre men" who had usurped the levers of power under the cover of parliamentary democracy.[12] The quest in *Sous l'œil des barbares* is implicitly linked to Barrès' hope that Boulanger would be able to renovate the national spirit and provide inspiration for the spiritually disgusted young generation. This novel, which is the most directly rooted in the schoolboy's world, is dominated by the obsession with the master. The double axis of revolt and quest which structures the successive *tableaux* of the young man's life is in its simplest form the rejection of the schoolmaster[13] and the search for the ideal master, the spiritual father who will provide a solution to the "problem of life." The master, who is so constantly the object of the young man's desire, turns out to be the Barbarian — the enemy of the Self — but nonetheless this novel is a testimony to the importance of the master-disciple relationship in Barrès' imagination. The "Oraison" which ends *Sous l'œil des barbares* is a cry for salvation: "O maître qui guérirait de la sécheresse" (SB. p. 271). The theme of the Barbarians is closely linked, then, to the adolescent revolt of

---

[12] "Boulangisme: Notes d'un lettré" in *L'Œuvre de Maurice Barrès*, I, 510.

[13] As Barrès later wrote in *L'Examen des trois romans idéologiques*, "Le Bonhomme Système" represents that "éducation désolée qu'avant toute expérience nous reçumes de nos maîtres" (p. 24).

the *lycéen* against the intellectual authority of his teachers. From the very beginning, the Barbarian is a schoolmaster-philosopher figure; he appears initially as M. de Rougemont, Daniel's mentor in *Nouvelle pour les rêveurs* and then as the "Bonhomme Système"[14] in the first chapter of *Sous l'œil des barbares* and as M. X... to whom Barrès' young hero administers a sound thrashing in the second part of the book. Of course, the most famous schoolmaster-Barbarian in Barrès' work is Bouteiller in *Les Déracinés*, a characterization of the real life Auguste Burdeau who was his teacher in Nancy.[15]

Barrès attached great importance to his relationship with his elders whom he tended to see as spiritual guides and initiators, and his early writing is often concerned with working out his attitude towards them. Most young writers begin their careers in this way, writing at first under the influence of their predecessors while striving to affirm their own style in reaction to them. But in Barrès' case, this tendency was particularly self-conscious, and he often deals explicitly with the problem in his books. His journalistic preoccupation with modern "psychology" carries over into his novels. *Sous l'œil des barbares* is in large part about the young man's reactions to the various philosophical outlooks and ways of feeling which he encounters as he grows up. Barrès' reactions range from passionate admiration to satirical rejection,

---

[14] The name is taken from one of the sections of Part Two of Renan's *Souvenirs d'enfance et de jeunesse* which is called "Le Bonhomme Système." The nickname "Système" was given by the local people to a solitary and rather mysterious old man who was often heard to use the word. Renan recognized in him a true sage, a man who, like the saintly Spinoza, lived in the pure and abstract realm of his noble thoughts. A disciple of the *philosophes*, he believed that God was the principle of rational order within the world and he loved humanity as the representative of reason on earth. He would reveal nothing of his past, but piecing together a few indications, Renan believed that this was, in fact, one of the revolutionary fanatics of the Jacobin religion of the Supreme Being. In *Œuvres complètes*, Calmann-Lévy, 1948, II, 775-778.

[15] Barrès did his year of *philo* in 1879-80 at the *lycée* in Nancy where Auguste Burdeau, a fervent Republican, a disciple of Kant, and the translator in France of Schopenhauer's works, was the very capable and often inspiring teacher. He was called to Paris to the *lycée* Louis-le-Grand and later became a Ferryist *député* and then *Président de la chambre*. Burdeau was, of course, the model for Bouteiller in *Les Déracinés* and *Leurs Figures*.

and although rejection may seem to dominate, we must not underestimate the strength of his desire to submit to the spiritual authority of others.

M. X... is a thinly disguised caricature of Ernest Renan. The similarity in tone between *Sous l'œil des barbares* and *Huit jours chez Monsieur Renan,* which was published a few months earlier, is striking. In both, Barrès emphasizes the sacerdotal worldliness of Renan, the strange combination of ascetic detachment and sensual indulgence, and the satisfactions of vanity which the historian derives from his own success. M. X... is described as a Pyrrhonian ("Causeur divin, maître qui institua des doubles à toutes les certitudes" [SB. p. 177]), echoing the accusation often levelled at Renan that his critical thought had undermined religious faith without proposing anything to replace it. A sentence in the editor's foreword to the third (1904) edition of the satirical brochure quotes Barrès as saying that he no longer feels it necessary to make excuses for the intoxicating effect which Renan's thought had had upon him and which had driven him to "give a lyrical thrashing to [his] master." [16] The reference to Chapter Four of *Sous l'œil des barbares* is clear.

It is Renan, then, who in the guise of M. X... is chosen to express the essence of that "Parisian education" which awaits the young man when he leaves the provinces for the capital. The lesson is much the same as that of the "Bonhomme Système": the Self is the only reality and the search for personal gratification, preferably of a "higher" nature, is the only reasonable rule of life in the face of universal relativism. However, M. X...'s counsels are adapted to the Parisian world of ambition, intrigue, and vanity. There was at least a kind of desolate idealism in the "Bonhomme Système"'s withdrawal, whereas M. X... cynically tailors his pessimistic view of the world to the needs of an energetic and ambitious young man. He advises him to choose a "speciality" (p. 183), not, as M. de Rougemont would have it, in order to find an intellectual escape from the horror of life, but in order to gain "notoriety" (p. 182) and to enjoy its fruits.

---

[16] *L'Œuvre de Maurice Barrès,* II, 308.

Barrès' relations with his *maîtres* were complex, and nowhere do we feel this complexity more than in the case of Renan. The desire to attach himself as a disciple to the authority of another leads to a violent rejection of those whose teaching disappoints his expectations. Renan was one of Barrès' favorite targets for satire, precisely because his thought was so attractive to him. Jacques Vier is right when he says that, if the influence of Taine dominates *Les Déracinés* and the doctrine of natural growth, it is Renan whose presence pervades *Le Culte du moi*.[17] His flowing, almost sensual style, his marvellous lucidity, his intellectual dilettantism balanced by a religious depth of feeling, and his considerable worldly success had a seductive attraction for the young Barrès.

When he saw Renan for the first time, in his early twenties and just embarked on a literary career in Paris, he was overwhelmed by the presence of the "great man."[18] Here was success, visibly and tangibly. If he is at such pains to expose the cynicism of M. X...'s formula for ambition, it is because, at that time, he was supremely ambitious. Although, of course, he was genuinely irritated by the great man's lofty detachment and his condescendingly protective urbanity, the "lyrical thrashing" is laid not so much on Renan himself, as on the impression that he made on the young writer.

There was undoubtedly much that Barrès disliked and rejected in Renan's thought, but there was also much that he retained. Like many young men of his generation, he was distrustful of Renan; he found his message ambiguous and he found the man too much marked by the intellectual atmosphere of the Second Empire. Although Renan had expressed belief in progress and faith in the people, he came to have doubts on both issues as the years went by, particularly after 1870, so that it seemed hard to know

---

[17] Jacques Vier, "Barrès et le culte du moi," *Archives des lettres modernes*, Nos. 10-11 (March-April, 1958), pp. 31-32. Vier writes that Renan's dilettantism and his particular form of scepticism which is always at the service of sensibility dominate *Le Culte du moi*.

[18] His fascination with Renan dates back to his early days in Paris, Some of the texts in *Huit jours* had been published in 1886 in *Le Voltaire* and they were inspired by a ten minute visit which he and his friend Le Goffic had paid on the historian in 1885.

quite what Renan believed. He remained an idealist, but increasingly he appeared to put off the moment when the Ideal could be realized. His growing distrust of the people led him to adopt an elitist attitude himself. Politically, he espoused a kind of liberal conservatism which must have seemed rather tepid to Barrès. Renan's ideas were stimulating, but not very exalting; they provided no basis for action in the world, only for contemplation. The dialogue between Renan and Chincholle at the beginning of *Le Jardin de Bérénice* makes this quite clear, for, in this novel which explores as one of its principal themes the opposition between contemplation and commitment, it is Renan who at the outset is the spokesman for contemplative withdrawal. Yet the fact remains that Renan helped to fashion one of the essential poles of Barrès' sensibility: the desire to possess the world through understanding, that is to say, from the distance of a detached, inner comprehension in which all the facets, all the contradictions, of the world coexist in one harmonious intellectual embrace.

Barrès was drawn also to the introspective Renan, to the author of *Souvenirs d'enfance et de jeunesse.* He admired the richness of Renan's inner life and the lucidity with which he had analyzed its complexities. He detected in the older man a kindred spirit; a sensitive, nervous, and delicately sensual personality, an egotist in the highest sense of the word, ambitious not for power, or wealth, or fame, but for self-fulfillment. Thus it is appropriate that it be M. X... who lays the foundations of the cult of the Self. It is M. X... who urges the young man to create a "thousand universes" (p. 181) in which to cultivate and enjoy the reflections of his own Self, and it is he who describes the world as an orchard, a term which announces the garden as the great Barresian image for the artificial universe. His insistence on the need for a formula and a method in pursuing one's ambition foreshadows the program which Philippe elaborates in *Un Homme libre.*[19] And it is to some extent from Renan that Barrès derives

---

[19] Chapter IV of *Un Homme libre,* "Examen de conscience," and particularly the section entitled "Examen physique," is prefigured by M. X...'s advice: "Dénombrez avec scrupule vos forces: votre santé, votre extérieur, vos relations" (p. 184).

his cult of ideas as sensuous entities, that higher form of dilettantism on which the creation of his universe is based.

Another fundamental feature of *Le Culte du moi* which bears the mark of Renan's influence is its religious atmosphere. Barrès was struck by the way this religious historian, in parting ways with the Catholic church, had achieved a carry over of the religious sensibility into other areas of spiritual life. It was in his writings that the younger writer could penetrate himself with a certain Hegelian sense of the Ideal both as the Divine and as something to be created in the future. And, of course, his style owes much to Renan: the tone of aristocratic elegance lightly touched with ironic disdain; the liking for sensuous, lyrical rhythms; and the brilliant exposition of ideas in a language that is at once witty, persuasive, intelligent, and subtle.

It is interesting to note how similar the situation in *Les Déracinés* is to that in *Sous l'œil des barbares;* the group of friends in the later novel look to Bouteiller to provide them not just with instruction, but with a key to open the secrets of the modern world. It is not so much what Bouteiller actually teaches them that has such an effect on the young men of Lorraine; it is the example of his success. It is because his own personal prestige exalts their ambition that his teaching is a form of corruption for the young. They go forth into the world with his image in their minds as a model to be imitated.

At the end of *Leurs Figures,* which continues the adventures of François Sturel in the world of Parisian political intrigue, Bouteiller and François meet in the grounds of Versailles where both have gone to meditate the lessons of the recent weeks. Despite the enmity which has separated them, Bouteiller feels an irresistible urge, in this moment of defeat, to greet his former student. As they do so, Bouteiller slips and for a few seconds Sturel holds him in his arms. In a moment of sudden fraternal tenderness, all their differences fall away, and the two men suddenly realize how much they have suffered from the fact that everything has conspired to prevent them being "a master and a disciple" to each other, as they had always secretly desired. Sturel understands that his hatred of Bouteiller has to be seen as a kind of "disappointed love."

Education is clearly one of Barrès' main concerns. The insistence of the theme in his works is in fact a reflection of a much wider preoccupation with the problem of education in this period of French intellectual history. The subject of Paul Bourget's *Le Disciple* (1889) is the moral responsibility of the teacher,[20] and in *L'Étape* (1902) the current polemic between lay Republican education and Catholic teaching is at the center of the novel. By showing the disastrous consequences on young people of atheistic and egalitarian instruction, even when it is accompanied by the highest sense of moral uprightness in the teacher, Bourget exposes the danger to society of a system of universal and abstract education which takes no account of the structural inequality of that society. His message is the same as Barrès' in *Les Déracinés*: education of the wrong kind or in excess of the real opportunities that young men will find in life can only lead to the creation of unhappy, unadapted, or even anti-social individuals.

The failure of an education, then, is the principle theme of *Sous l'œil des barbares* and *Les Déracinés*. The cult of the self which is developed in *Un Homme libre* is an attempt to find a substitute within the inner "universe" of the egotist. Philippe looks to his intercessors and to Lorraine and Italy to provide him with a series of lessons as he advances along the path of self-perfection. The subtitle of Chapter IX "Veillée d'Italie" is "Enseignement du Vinci." Chapter VII of *Le Jardin de Bérénice is called* "La pédagogie de Bérénice," and indeed the whole novel is the account of what Philippe learns in her garden. Barrès uses exactly the same formula in *L'Ennemi des lois* where it is the Slavic "princess" Marina who is entrusted with the political and social education of André Maltère. *Le Culte du moi* and the more personal works which follow it at regular intervals throughout his life constitute an on-going pedagogy of the Self, while *Le Roman de l'énergie*

---

[20] In the name of Science and psychological experimentation, Robert Greslou coldly arouses a burning passion in the heart of an innocent and unsuspecting young girl. When she realizes that he has only been playing a grisly game, she kills herself in despair. Adrien Sixte, Robert's teacher, is shattered by this sudden irruption of real life into his abstract world. It is tragically brought home to him that a teacher is responsible not just for the precision and efficiency of his students' minds, but also for the uses to which they put their science.

nationale, Les Bastions de l'Est, and the group of propagandistic books are an attempt to widen his enquiry to the life of the nation as a whole.

The meaning of *Un Homme libre* is put into better perspective when we realize that Philippe is seeking not only liberation, but a faith to which he may apply his life in a spirit of submission. It is in the absence of faith and in the interim, as it were, while he is constructing a new one, that the young man affirms the absolute liberty of the Self. Yet he desires a mentor whose teaching would release his enthusiasm, channel his energies, and employ his sense of duty and his need to obey. Barrès is looking for a cure for the spiritual sickness which seems to be the heritage of the century. Towards the end of *Sous l'œil des barbares,* the young man hopes to find salvation in a formula for action, because he has understood that his impotence stems from his spiritual isolation.

The principal source of despair in the sensibility of the *poète maudit,* the Decadent, the Symbolist, or the *fin de siècle* pessimist is his separation from the world and his awareness that dream and action can no longer coincide. He is condemned to the sterile world of his own mind. His imagination is no longer enmeshed in reality and his excessive cerebrality operates in a vacuum, endlessly analyzing the varying states of his soul. Desire is turned to illusory and ephemeral ends which have no contact with the real world, and consciousness is heightened to the point of suffering. Impotence and the failure of desire are thus two of the most persistent themes of the 19th century.

We can see in this condition and in the attempt to find a remedy for it the origin of a certain paradox in the program of the egotist. On the one hand, given the total collapse of faith in his age, he can find no other expression for his creative energies than to cultivate his own inner universe, and this he proceeds to do, arrogantly and in defiance of all other men. The cult of the self is simply an extreme and systematic development of the spirit of the times. On the other hand, the egotist is trying to achieve for himself a therapy and a pedagogy which will lead him back to the world; and for this he must find a basis of conviction and certainty on which he can ground his action. His appeal to the *maître* in the "Oraison" is not for more knowledge or better analyses of the situation, but for a much more essential spiritual aid. Faith, health, energy, and the strength to act and to will, these are the values for which the young man longs. "Toi seul, o maître, si tu existes quelque part, axiome, religion ou prince des hommes" (p. 279).

If Barrès had been born forty years later, he would have been the most fervent of Gaullists. His tragedy was that he lived in a time when political leaders were so uninspiring, caught up as they were in the unedifying maneuvering of parliamentary democracy under the Third Republic. But, of course, this is putting things the wrong way round. The point is rather that Barrès, reacting against the unglorious spectacle of public life in France after 1870, helped to create a way of thinking, feeling, and speaking from which Gaullism emerged. However this may be, the expression "prince des hommes" calls to mind General Boulanger who for a while in the late eighties sparked the popular imagination.[21] Here was a man who seemed to promise energetic leadership, a dynamic vision of national destiny, and a clean sweep of the political board. For Barrès, he was particularly attractive because he allied the prestige of the army to an ability to stir the masses. He saw in the spontaneous support which arose for Boulanger an expression of the collective will of the French people and for this reason he felt that Boulangism was an authentic national movement. From what we know of Barrès' liking for instinctual energy and his desire for action, it is not hard to imagine how he must have been drawn to a movement which claimed to be populist and which proposed a regeneration of national life.

The appeal to the *maître* at the end of *Sous l'œil des barbares* has, then, a certain literal meaning. The theme is rooted in Barrès' relations with his own schoolteachers and he does seem to have desired a flesh and blood incarnation of the spiritual guidance

---

[21] After obtaining a sweeping success in the elections of January 27th, 1889, General Boulanger failed to follow up a strategic advantage which could have overthrown the Third Republic. There seems little doubt that, had he acted, the regime of President Carnot could not have withstood the assault. On April 1st, 1889, he fled to Brussels and in 1891 he shot himself on the grave of his mistress. See D. W. Brogan, *The Development of Modern France*, 1870-1939, Volume I *(From the Fall of the Empire to the Dreyfus Affair)*.

that he invokes. The tone and sense of the novel are predominantly negative, however, and it is evident from the interrogative ending that the young man has not found his guiding principle. What he has discovered is the strength of his desire and the fact that nothing which has been presented to him can satisfy it. Yet there is a kind of strength in despair; the very urgency of his desire is in itself a source of energy. The "Oraison" serves both as a conclusion to *Sous l'œil des barbares* in that it is the total realization by its hero of his spiritual solitude, thereby completing the process of rejection and disentanglement, and a transition to *Un Homme libre* in which the quest for self-possession is given an explicitly religious framework.

The young man satisfies his need for passionate admiration in the cult of what he calls his intercessors. Benjamin Constant and Charles-Augustin Sainte-Beuve serve as inspirational examples with which Philippe in *Un Homme libre* can partly identify. Literature provides him with interim lay saints as he pursues his quest for a faith. The voices of Lorraine and Venice are joined to those of the intercessors in this provisional stage of self-fortification. Deprived of a master, Philippe learns to turn the objects of his own enthusiasm into sources of moral instruction. The notion of the "universe" — by which the Self creates the world in its own image for its own enjoyment and edification — is evidently a solipsism. The young egotist applies to the Cult of his own Self the sense of duty, the need to serve, and the impulses of noble heroism which were thwarted in the external world.

The next step is to ground the individual ego in the wider existence of the group. This allows Barrès to transform egotism (seen at first as a sense of duty to the creative energy of the solitary self) into a social morality. In serving the true interests of his own ego, he is at the same time furthering the development of the group. Thus he is able, in each movement of self-affirmation, to assert the complete liberty of the individual ego and a reassuring sense of necessity. Barrès is able to affirm his difference and his identity simultaneously. He strives to internalize the authority he needs to order and discipline his energies. The Self, being a continuation of its ancestors and a particle of that larger entity constituted by the nation, is obeying the principles of its own existence when it submits to the determinism of *La Terre et les morts.* He replaces the desired external authority by his own doctrine elaborated in conformity with his own being. And having erected this body of dogma, he proceeds to submit to it as if it were an objective faith. In the absence of a master and a leader, Barrès becomes his own disciple.

Another consequence of this assumption within the Self of the role of the *maître* is that, in addition to being his own teacher, Barrès becomes a preceptor for his public. He transforms the world into a series of object lessons for his own and his readers' edification. At the beginning of the *Examen des trois romans idéologiques*, written several years after *Le Culte du moi*, he makes a statement that is essential to an understanding of his work. "Toute grande poésie est un enseignement, je veux que l'on me considère comme un maître ou rien" (p. 13).

"Un maître ou rien" — certainly his public and his critics did not disappoint him in this regard, for his readers were first and foremost his disciples. Much of the early criticism devoted to Barrès was of the "hommage to the master" type.[22] However, the main point that I wish to make here is that the spirit in which his readers received his message is in itself indicative of the intellectual atmosphere in which he developed the theme of the *maître*. There was at the end of the century a general trend towards doctrine and discipline as a reaction against the relativism and the nihilism which were feared by so many. In a period marked by excessive individualism, the search for spiritual order, and just as essentially for spiritual community, took many forms. Barrès' nationalism, in its rhetorical and literary form, had great appeal because it satisfied the need for collective identity, while retaining the "romantic" values of individual plenitude, diffuse religiosity, and spiritualized estheticism.

Barrès' early works are nearly all structured around one basic situation. A young man, faced with a philosophical or politico-philosophical problem which he must solve in order to decide on

---

[22] The title of René Jacquet's book, *Notre Maître Maurice Barrès* (1900), is indicative of this reverential strain of criticism. Other suggestive titles are Frédéric Empaytaz, *Reconnaissance à Barrès* (1925), Henri Gouhier, *Notre ami Barrès* (1928), and even Pierre de Boisdeffre's *Barrès parmi nous* (1952).

the conduct of his life, is placed between the dialectical poles of two very different ways of apprehending the world. On the one hand, there is a young woman who represents sensibility, intuition, the heart, and instinctive understanding, and on the other a philosopher figure, who is often also the Adversary or the Barbarian, incarnating the male characteristics of reason, objectivity, and, sometimes, unfeeling calculation.

In *Nouvelle pour les rêveurs,* Daniel Camille is torn between the teaching of the philosopher, M. de Rougemont, his friend and counsellor, and the example of his niece, Madame de Railles. He learns from the wise old man that it was an error on the part of earlier generations to look for happiness in emotion. Only the intelligence, by detaching us from life and replacing emotion by understanding can lead to true peace and acceptance. It is better and nobler to pursue the idea of things than to lead a life of action in which we can only suffer. The wise man is he who lives above the "vile reality" of the world. However, the old man's teaching is contradicted in the person of his niece, Madame de Railles. After a great personal tragedy — the death of her husband and the loss of her fortune — her uncle had taken her into his household. In contrast to the detachment and lucidity of the old man, she incarnates naked sensibility. Her whole being is engulfed in sorrow and in melancholy remembrance of the past. She reacts to life with the unreasoning instinctiveness of emotion, finding consolation in the sad beauty of autumn and in the tears that she is so easily moved to shed.

Although Monsieur de Rougemont is much more sympathetically drawn than his descendants in *Sous l'œil des barbares,* it is evident that this story is a prototype of Barrès' early fiction. The same dialectical movement that we find in the philosophical framework of this story underlies all his thought: the antitheses of contemplation and passionate involvement, reason and sensibility, life felt as an instinctive passion projected into the future and death seen as a negation of every moment (the *Qualis artifex pereo* of *Le Jardin de Bérénice*). Around the contrasting figures of Mme de Railles and Daniel, Barrès ponders the mystery of time in human sensibility, torn between nostalgia for the past and desire for the future. And it is interesting to note that in this, one of the earliest of his texts, we find the same dialogue between reason and the instinctual forces of the heart as in *La Colline inspirée,* where, towards the end of his career, he undoubtedly gave the most intense expression to these themes. Again, one can discern in these pages the beginning of his life-long meditation upon the dual virtues of detached intellectual understanding and passionate acceptance of the creative life forces as different modes of possessing the world. Most of the elements of Barrès' sensibility are present in *Nouvelle pour les rêveurs:* the feverish melancholy, the voluptuousness of pathos and pity, the excited juxtaposition of sensuality and death, and the nervous lucidity of the male character.

The protagonists in this story appear in many forms in the books that follow, but the schema is the same. Mme de Railles becomes the *amie* of *Sous l'oeil des barbares,* Bérénice in the third volume of the trilogy, Marina in *L'Ennemi des lois,* and then Simone in *Un Amateur d'âmes.* Monsieur de Rougemont becomes "Le Bonhomme Système" and M. X... in *Sous l'œil des barbares,* then Charles Martin, the Adversary in *Le Jardin de Bérénice.* The Barbarians, who are perhaps best defined as the enemies of the heart, are represented in *L'Ennemi des lois* by the vivisectionists at whose hands Marina's beloved dog is almost destroyed. However, in this book, the philosophical dimension of the dialectic is no longer incarnated in one character; the opposition here is between Marina and the political ideologies among which André Maltère attempts to achieve a clearer understanding of the conditions for social harmony.

The fictional element in his early works is a kind of self-allegory similar to the basic model of *Nouvelle pour les rêveurs.* They are constructed as a three-way debate between Barrès and another, usually feminine side of himself, and between these two and the potentially menacing forces of the outside world. The representation of himself, either in the third person as the young man in *Sous l'œil des barbares* and as André Maltère in *L'Ennemi des lois,* or in the first person as Philippe in *Un Homme libre* and *Le Jardin de Bérénice,* is the reflective side of his being — not merely intelligence in contrast to sensibility, but rather that higher part of the Self where sensibility and reflection are synthesized. The young men are mostly passive in the novels. They stand outside many of the events, personally uninvolved, but participating in them vicariously through the reactions of the young women.

Les Déracinés is no different from *Le Culte du moi* in this respect. The story of the seven school friends who come from Nancy to Paris to find success and fortune draws on the same personal experience and illustrates the same themes as the trilogy. The solitary individual has been replaced by the group, but the adventures of these young men, troubled by the teaching of their philosophy teacher in Nancy and searching for a way to integrate themselves into the life of their country, constitute a *Bildungsroman* which, although superficially in the tradition of Balzac, Stendhal, and Flaubert, is really just an adaptation to the naturalist mode of this basic Barresian situation.

Although Barrès abandoned this kind of allegorical treatise novel of his early writing, the same three-way structural pattern continues throughout his work. His books are almost all dialectically constructed. He tends to establish a dialogue between his reflective Self and an incarnation of his own sensibility. After *Le Jardin de Bérénice,* he makes an increasing use of landscape to reflect the profound layers of his soul. In this novel, the landscapes are extensions of Bérénice and the harmony between the two is such that they both convey the same message. In his later writings, it is often the landscapes alone that serve as the second element in his dialectical meditations. Or it is Lorraine that takes over the role played by his heroines in the early novels, assuming most of their characteristics: battered nobility, a tragic sense of the past, a heroic stoicism in the face of humiliation and suffering, and a mysterious, melancholy profundity of being which inspires emotions of pity and pathos in the heart of the observer. Sensibility is portrayed as a dolorous relation to the world. It is a passive, defenseless suffering destined to endure the loss and the humiliations imposed by the cruel world. The basic model, which I am concerned with here, is most completely realized when the woman succombs to her sufferings and to the oppression of the outside world. This is the case in *Le Jardin de Bérénice* where Bérénice, forced to marry the unfeeling Charles Martin, withers and dies.

The andversary relationship to that part of the world which cannot be assimilated to the Self is one the constants in Barrès' works. The psychological situation of opposition and reaction is shifted from the individual to the political plane in the later works: the sensitive side of himself is identified with the nation or the province, while the enemies of the Self may become quite simply Germany in this geo-political transfer of his own drama. The relation of the occupied territories to the German invader in *Les Bastions de l'est* is exactly the same as that of Bérénice to Charles Martin. Making allowances for the fact that *Colette Baudoche* is a work of propaganda framed in a naturalist mode, one can see that the heroine of this novel is herself a descendant of the heroines of the allegorical novels.

The persistence of this situation in Barrès' books reflects the depth of anxiety underlying the theme of the Barbarians. The vulnerable, sensitive Self feels tragically threatened by everything that is alien to it. The theme of the adversary is an expression of his feeling that his relation with the outside world is one of opposition and confrontation, and that his first duty to himself is to adopt a protective attitude. In the *Examen,* he links his definition of the Barbarians to the theory of the Self. They are all those that interfere with the growth of the Self in any way. In this sense, they are the Non-Self, all that is harmful or opposed to the authentic being. The young man first comes to be conscious of himself in a spontaneous, yet thoroughly negative reaction of disgust and uneasiness in what he feels to be a hostile world. The self-awareness is vague at first, but its development is linked to the tendency of our deepest instincts to recoil from all unnatural interference and to set up mechanisms of defense. Spiritual progress begins as reaction and negation for Barrès. The Barbarians, the adverse forces of the world, are the first instruments of self-consciousness and they remain an important and permanent feature of his particular form of self-assertion which depends on the clear designation of what it is drawn up against: the alien, the adversary, the Non-Self. The adversary relationship is from the beginning an essential part of the dynamics of egotism by which the Self affirms itself in opposition.

CHAPTER II

THE CONQUEST OF ENERGY

I. *Sensibility*

Barrès' awareness of his own existence, of his own difference and specific virtue, was born of a negative reaction against those who tried to fashion his being. He was driven, then, to construct heroic dreams or to devise disdainful poses in order to protect himself "under the eye of the Barbarians." Throughout all the young man's experiences in *Sous l'œil des barbares,* he was guided by an ideal to which he would not give any mediocre expression. This ambition was the complete realization of his potential for experiencing the world and a determination to remain faithful to the authentic being whose presence he felt in the depths of his sensibility.

It will be remembered that the quest in *Sous l'œil des barbares* turned up only one truth: the rather sad conclusion that the Self is the only reality. As a result, reality, for Barrès' egotist, is constituted by the succession of sensations and emotions. This being the case, the supreme good is the most intense sensation, not only because it gives pleasure, but also because it brings with it the impression of power and freedom. Emotion is apprehended by his characters as quality and potency, that is, as *value* in itself. But this sense of value is as ephemeral as the emotion which gives rise to it. Emotion is threatened by time which sweeps away all our privileged moments in the rhythm of change and loss which makes up our consciousness. Barrès will not be content just to be the dilettante of his own emotions. His project is to ground permanent values on feeling and consciousness. But how can ephemeral emotion be converted into something having that permanence which he so desired?

The attempt to achieve this transition or conversion is a constant feature of his work. In its fundamental impulse, it is the passage from feeling to being. It is expressed in the concern to transform emotion into thought, that is, to transform the fleeting moments of existence into an essential continuity of the mind. In terms of value, it is the desire to turn unstable emotion into a source of spiritual energy which can be accumulated in the soul. Barrès returns time and time again in his works to the idea of "reservoirs" or "deposits" of emotion from which he derives spiritual strength. His endeavor is to harness the energy generated by his own enthusiasm. The first step is to seek out the occasions for experiencing intense emotions while bringing them to a maximum of consciousness. This is stated in the axiom that Philippe and Simon derive from their visit to Jersey: "Il faut sentir le plus possible en analysant le plus possible" (HL. p. 10). The second step is the essential one in his system, and by far the hardest. He must find a way to create soul substance out of his experiences, and it is from this effort that his doctrine is to evolve.

Before I discuss Barrès' method and its objectives in more detail, I wish to consider the dynamics of this sensibility which is the starting point of the Cult of the Self. The exposition of feeling is one of the main constituents of his work, which tends as a result to be organized around certain moments of *rêverie* and meditation. Nearly always in these texts, there is an outward and upward movement towards what one might call an ideal state of plenitude. In this, he is again quite typical of his century; there are many writers who use literature to create an ideal state of physical and spiritual awareness. We only have to think of the poems by Baudelaire or Verlaine in which complexes of impressions, descriptions, and sensations constitute a vision of an ideal dimension of existence. Such states are in the last analysis only realizable in literature; which no doubt explains the great spiritual demands put upon it in the 19th century.

In Chapter Two of *Sous l'œil des barbares*, there is a description of such a *rêverie*, evoking a moment of sexual plenitude in the hero's adolescence. The young man and his companion are wandering aimlessly through Barrès' symbolist landscape, he in search of wisdom and she in the hope of seducing the young Narcissus. Here is the text:

> Ils atteignirent lentement au sommet de la colline, sous un ciel de lune rougissant. Ce profond paysage d'où affleuraient des branches raides et la plainte monotone des campagnes noyées dans la nuit, fut-il si enchanteur, ou leurs âmes avaient-elles atteint ces équilibres furtifs que parfois réalisent deux illusions entrelacées; brûlaient-elles de cette ardeur intime qui vaporise toute inquiétude? Qu'importe le mot de leur fièvre dévorante! Parmi cette tendresse du soir, sur les gazons onctueux, dans le silence pénétrant et la fraîcheur féconde, la même allégresse, en leurs poitrines allégées d'un même poids, rhythmait leurs pensées et leur sang; et c'est ainsi qu'étendus côte à côte, sans se mouvoir, sans un soupir, yeux perdus dans la nuit d'argent que toujours on regrettera sous la pluie dorée de midi, ils ne furent plus qu'un frissonnement du bonheur impersonnel. — Nuances des musiques très lointaines qui fondez les plus ténues subtilités! limites où notre vie qui va s'affaisser déjà ne se connaît plus! seules peut-être effleurez-vous la douceur mystique de toutes ces choses oubliées (pp. 99-100).

In spite of its juvenile lyricism, the text is interesting because it contains elements which recur in many of Barrès' exaltations. We can ignore the stylistic coquetteries and the picturesque details of the setting, frequent in the early chapters of *Sous l'œil des barbares*, but which tend to disappear after Chapter Three: expressions like *ciel de lune rougissant, gazons onctueux*. And *illusions entrelacées, vaporise toute inquiétude, ténues subtilités, toutes ces choses oubliées* remind us that this passage is related to the themes of illusory appearance, relativity, and uncertainty which characterize the life of the mind as the young man discovers it in the Temple of Wisdom. Nonetheless, the reader is immediately struck by a typically Barresian tonality and cadence: the solemnity of the passage, reinforced by the *passé simple* in a sentence like *ils ne furent plus qu'un bonheur impersonnel!* the exclamatory lyricism; the precise complexity of the syntax in the expression of a vague and subtle state of exaltation; the series of verbless appositional phrases at the end of the development; and the suggestion of a musical and mystical dimension of the experience. The text is composed in the 19th century tradition (perfected by Baudelaire) in which the adjective and the abstract noun specify the spiritual value of the sensations. Thus the ideal quality of the *rêverie à deux* is translated by such words as *profond, enchanteur, ardeur, pénétrant, féconde*. There are perhaps certain Verlainian echoes in this soft nocturnal landscape — *plainte monotone, campagnes noyées* — but monotony is one of the attributes that nearly all Barrès' landscapes have, although more often it is accompanied by the idea of severity. Profundity, ardor, and fecundity are essential qualities of his ideal projections, though one can probably say that they are common to all ecstatic experiences. However, there are two elements which become truly distinguishing features in his works — the *fièvre* and the *frissonnement* which convey a very special state of nervous mental excitement. *Bonheur impersonnel* is associated with the Nirvanist themes of the first part of the novel, but it is characteristic of Barrès in as much as it reveals a feeling of communion through emotion with some vast spiritual reality beyond himself.

The harmony achieved in this text has a rather tenuous quality, however. It is not just the fact that the two lovers remain essentially separated — this is always the case when a sexual relationship is portrayed in Barrès' books. The disquieting thing is that the harmony is realized at an extreme point at which consciousness almost fades into oblivion. Throughout the text he has developed the idea of uncertainty and indistinctness. Like the landscape itself, they are immersed *(noyées)* in the night, *yeux perdus,* and the limiting *ils ne furent plus qu'un ...* strengthens this idea. Their consciousness is drawn out of themselves as it were, towards those frontiers *(limites)* where they are hardly aware of their existence *(où notre vie ... ne se connaît plus)*. The image of far-away strains of music suggests this notion of distance. Barrès' *rêverie* fixes the movement of emotion on its downswing as it descends towards an ecstatic annihilation. This association of sexual desire and dissolution of consciousness was quite commonplace in the 19th century — in Wagner's music and in the poetry of Baudelaire or Verlaine for example. When we remember the program of *Un Homme libre:* "Sentir le plus possible," we understand how great a danger this temptation represents for the egotist. One of Barrès' great desires was undoubtedly for a harmonious union with the universe, but for a union in which he would retain maximum consciousness.

Sometimes, in their initial upsurge, the emotions of his characters have a powerful expansive drive. They are overwhelmed by a Dionysiac intoxication; it is as if their faculties were being multiplied as they project themselves omnipotently upon the world. But these emotions tend to exhaust themselves, either as a result of some inherent principle of desire itself or as a result of a sudden rational awareness which destroys the illusion. The following text from *L'Ennemi des lois* illustrates the first tendency. André Maltère is visiting Venice with his mistress Marina and, shortly after their arrival there, they listen rapturously to the music of Verdi under the magnificent September sky.

> Ce lui était une sensualité aussi accablante que les pleurs ou les spasmes de sa maîtresse, de frémir et s'apitoyer avec tout ce peuple dans une belle légende de la Venise passionnée. Ivre de beauté forte et de l'éclat de tous ces garçons et filles nés pour les caresses, il s'enfonçait hors de soi-même dans une mollesse où il eût voulu confondre et évanouir tous les sexes de toutes les races, qui pullulent et tourbillonnent de désir sur la face de la terre (pp. 100-101).

The choice of the word "sensuality," rather than "pleasure" or "joy," is significant in describing his reactions to the mingling of the beauty of the music and the beauty of Venice. This sensuality is overwhelming *(accablante)*, by which Barrès suggests the impossibility of satisfying his desire. This frustration is felt as a bodily sensation, an affliction of the nerves betrayed by tears and spasms. The emotion is reduced to the thrill of the body and sexual overtones are added by the analogy with his mistress.

The physical unease develops into an almost apocalyptical urge for sexual union which would join the sexes of all races in one cosmic orgasm. The words which convey this exaltation suggest a frenzied Dionysiac force which would consume itself and the entire universe: *ivre, éclat, s'enfonçait, pullulent, tourbillonnent,* while sexual appeasement is evoked in terms of annihilation, a return to the warm, soft oblivion of chaos — *une mollesse où il eût voulu confondre et évanouir* ... Hence sexual release is equated with Death, with forgetfulness of Self. The psychic charge of tension created by his enthusiasm is not released, however, but the intensity drops and André falls into that state of feverish exhaustion which was also the sickness of Philippe. It is the lassitude of unsatisfied, impossible desire; his nerves are shattered and his sensibility dulled. He is the victim of a kind of postcoital sadness which is, however, devoid of the accompanying calm and renewal.

At other moments, it is not so much the inner dynamics of desire which threaten to undermine the experience, but the cold shock of reason. When Philippe reaches the highest point of the Tour Constance above the walls of Aigues-Mortes, he is filled with an expansive melancholy at the spectacle of the vast sweep of sea and marsh which seems to correspond exactly to the infinite reach of his desires (JB. p. 67). However, he is soon checked by the thought that his own existence is only a transitory moment in the universe. He reflects that his emotion will disappear like that of the hundreds of other people who have stood on that same spot and felt that they too were united for a brief moment with the view before them. The awareness of time passing is the worm in the bud which makes it impossible for Philippe to give himself entirely to the ecstatic possession of the present moment. However, it must also be noted that the moral suffering which often appears as the second phase of Barrès' *rêveries* is in itself a value. There is a melancholy, yet positive, pleasure in the lucid awareness of finitude and death. In fact, it is precisely this lucidity that he comes more and more to prize and cultivate. It is the starting point for the final constructive phase of his meditations in which the initial emotion is converted into "ideology." Emotion provides an impetus to the highly abstract, analytic, and intellectual imagination that is the mark of Barrès' originality. This imagination functions best in moments of psychic tension, when moral suffering produces exactly that acuity of consciousness which is the Barresian ideal. So, paradoxically, it is the feeling of loss, failure, or inadequacy which allows him to achieve what he fails to achieve in the movement of emotion itself: that is, a passionate consciousness of all his riches. The fact that this is accompanied by an equally lucid awareness of his limits does not lessen the value of the experience, especially since it will be the role of the constructive imagination to create the conditions for a feeling of security. Such values as lucidity, concentrated self-awareness, solidity, and permanence have to be seen as the counterparts of a dangerous penchant towards expansion and mobility.

There are texts in Barrès' work which suggest that he is naturally inclined to seek a spontaneous contact with the outside world. Indeed, we shall see that spontaneity is one of the principal ideological values in *Le Jardin de Bérénice* and *L'ennemi des lois*. But although there is a definite cult of the privileged moments, he is not drawn along the path of impressionism. In this he stands apart from a current which, through the Goncourts, Vallès, Loti, and many other *Romanciers de l'instantané* as Jacques Dubois[1] calls them, was gathering strength in the last decades of the 19th century. And while one can find a certain influence upon Gide of Barrès' idea of the therapeutic value of sensation, he is far from giving the same importance to the present instant that Gide does in *Les Nourritures terrestres*. And he is at the antipodes of those writers who, in the 20th century, celebrated the eternity of the present moment or *la vie immédiate* of the Surrealists, even though one can observe in his work a theoretical glorification of vital forces. He will not risk that confusion with the material world, that objectification of the Self which is a source of joy for some modern sensibilities. In a movement of self-preservation, he opposes the Self rigorously to the world and defends the separate consciousness from any spontaneous identification with it.

Whatever the dangers inherent in emotion, it is still the cornerstone of the awareness of the Self as value. The purpose of linking emotion to lucid consciousness is not to replace emotion by lucidity, but to maintain it, to prevent it from dissipating into thin air and leaving nothing to be "put in reserve," as Barrès says of the emotions created by the facile romanticism of music (SB. p. 257). However, this state of enthusiasm is threatened by another danger which arises from the nature of lucidity itself. The analytic faculty, which he seeks to attach to feeling, tends to

---

[1] Jacques Dubois, *Les Romanciers français de l'instantané*, Bruxelles, Palais des Académies, 1963. Particularly the Goncourt brothers, Alphonse Daudet, Jules Vallès, and Pierre Loti.

destroy emotion in its own way. We see this in the last chapter of *Sous l'œil des barbares* when the young man's exaltation collapses into despair.

In Chapter Six we find him alone in his room late at night, smoking a huge cigar[2] and overtaken gradually by a delicious abstract *rêverie* which is characteristically *indefinite* and *powerful* (p. 232). The intense feeling fires his imagination and his cerebral processes so that he rises above the usual limitations of consciousness to achieve a sense of the unity of the Self in harmony with the outside world. At the same time he goes beyond the classifications of mere understanding to an impression of the absolute. As we might expect, this feeling does not last. In Chapter Seven the young man is unsuccessfully trying to play the game of living according to the rules of the "majority" (p. 261), while hiding his true self from the eyes of the world. The strain is too much for him; he is uneasy, dissatisfied, and bitter. He feels impotent to remedy his own despair or to assert his ideal. He no longer has that feeling of power over his own psychic mechanism which is so essential for the egotist. He realizes that he has lost his capacity for enthusiasm partly because he is so introspective: "Je me touchai avec ingéniosité de mille traits aigus d'analyse" (p. 265), "J'ai trop voulu me subtiliser" (p. 266). He blames his "detestable lucidities and expansions" (p. 268) for the state in which he finds himself. When his enthusiasm drops, he is left with cold abstractions and pointless subtleties. The mechanism continues to turn but it produces only a feeling of feverish anguish:

> Ah! cette sécheresse! ces harassements de reprendre, à froid et d'une âme rétrécie, des théories qui hier m'échauffaient! Ah! presser une imagination, systématiser, syn-

---

[2] This is perhaps a reminiscence of Baudelaire's *Journaux intimes* (see also pages 120-21 of this chapter and note 16). At the end of Fusées, Baudelaire meditates on the bourgeois hell which surrounds him from the isolation of his room: "Perdu dans ce vilain monde, coudoyé par les foules, je suis comme un homme lassé.... Le soir où cet homme a volé à sa destinée quelques heures de plaisir, bercé dans sa digestion, oublieux —autant que possible— du passé, content du présent et résigné à l'avenir, enivré de son sang-froid et son dandysme, fier de n'être pas aussi bas que ceux qui passent, il se dit en contemplant la fumée de son cigare: Que m'importe où vont ces consciences?" (*Œuvres complètes*, Gallimard, "Bibliothèque de la Pléiade," 1961, pp. 1264-65).

thétiser, éliminer, affiner, comparer! besogne d'écœurement! dégoût! d'où l'on atteint la stérilité (p. 244).

Sterility (or *sécheresse*) is probably the principal threat to the egotist's possession of the universe. The contraction of his soul *(une âme rétrécie)* is the exact opposite of the infinite expansion to which exaltation had led him. The feeling is one of coldness and physical disgust in which the emotional faculties are dessicated.

The tension at the center of Barrès' work is that of the conscious self separated from its world. His desire is for integration, unity, and harmony; but this can only be achieved in what he calls "a state of grace": that is, in sustained enthusiasm. If ecstasy is the psychic charging of the outside world as emotional value, depression is the inability to bridge the gap between the self and the world. Reality becomes colorless, a collection of meaningless phenomena; the world is no longer perceived in its harmony, but as fragmentation. It is a multiplicity of dead objects which the intelligence can order, classify, and synthesize, but which refuse themselves to the heart. The feeling of sterility is often rendered by words which evoke the cold lifelessness of statistics, the automatic functioning of the analytic mind no longer fired (*échauffé* in Barrès' vocabulary) by emotion. When he wishes to condemn Charles Martin, the engineer in *Le Jardin de Bérénice*, for the sterility of his approach to life, he shows him labelling with their exact names the waters, trees, and vegetation of the country around Aigues-Mortes (p. 72). To characterize Karl Marx and other Jewish intellectuals, he writes that they manipulate ideas as a banker manipulates securities (EL, p. 144). Barrès was always the enemy of purely intellectual understanding.

In the last analysis, the internal enemies of the Self are the presence of death in the soul and in its world. The death of the relative and the finite, the spiritual death of the world when its multiplicity is lifeless separation, and above all the death of emotion which alone is capable of fusing the fullness of life into the universe.

> Cette mort perpétuelle, ce manque de continuité de nos émotions, voilà ce qui désole l'égotiste et marque l'échec de sa prétention (JB. p. 181).

The finite being, reduced to realizing its theoretically limitless potential successively, one by one, despairs of achieving the unitary harmony of which he dreams. In *Un Homme libre,* Philippe speaks of the "impression which constitutes (his) anguish: the sense of the provisional" (p. 175). The present is ephemeral change, the point where death is continually inserted into life, so Barrès seeks a permanence beyond the succession of mortal instants. "Se construire un univers permanent" — this was the great task that he set himself in his life and in his writing, and the first step was to distinguish a permanent, absolute Self from the contingent, mortal Self.

II. *The Self and the World*

At the beginning of *Sous l'œil des Barbares,* Barrès employs the popular figure of Narcissus to represent the young man's "self-consciousness." It is his propensity for introspection which, by making him recoil from the sollicitations of the outside world, leads him to an awareness of an inner Self. The vague aspiration towards an unknown Ideal takes the form of inner directed desire. In Chapter Two, the Girl allegorizes the sensual attraction of the world. She offers the possibility of a spontaneous satisfaction of his desire, but he prefers his melancholy *rêverie* to union with her. When she tries to seduce him by undressing before him, he rejects her completely because he is afraid that he would lose himself in the passion of love. "Souffrez que je ne m'échappe pas à moi-même" (5B p. 97), he exclaims. One of Barrès' principal goals in *Le Culte du moi,* and in all his writing, is to safeguard the integrity of his being. By his narcissistic assertion of the Self, his desire is directed, not outwards where it would risk losing itself, but inwards onto his own consciousness. This pure awareness of Self in opposition to the attractions of the universe is similar to that elaborated by Paul Valéry; in his poem "Fragments du Narcisse" for example he writes:

> J'y trouve un tel trésor d'impuissance et d'orgueil,
>
> Que nulle vierge enfant échappée au satyre,
> Nulle! aux fuites habiles, aux chutes sans émoi,
> Nulle des nymphes, nulle amie, ne m'attire

Comme tu fais sur l'onde, inépuisable Moi! [3]

Again in *La Jeune Parque*, pure consciousness is opposed to the demands of the senses for harmony with the universe.

Barrès gives the Narcissus myth a meaning quite different from the one it has traditionally. For him, Narcissism is a positive impulse rather than a moral tragedy in which the adolescent's fascination with his beauty dissolves his being in the shimmering unreality of his reflection in the water. In fact, he has completely reserved the usual significance of the story, for loss of Self is no longer seen to be the result of confusing oneself with one's own image but of confusing oneself with the outside world. The passivity of Narcissus' impossible yearning becomes an active principle of self-discovery in Barrès' system. The manner in which he takes over the myth with its usual negative meaning and bends it to his own purposes is quite typical of the spirit of *Le Culte du moi*. The whole enterprise is after all a kind of provocation. Egoism and self-love are not normally held up as virtues, even less as axioms for founding a system. There is much deliberate impertinence in his brazen assertion of the "me only" and the "me first."

Thus Narcissism is a creative defense of the Self at a moment when the egotist is clinging to consciousness of his difference as a first step in the dialectic of self-development. In another part of this same episode with the Loved One in Chapter Two, Barrès introduces an idea to which he often returns in *Le Culte du moi*. By giving absolute priority to the separateness of his own identity, he reduces the outside world to indifferent Otherness in which Objects, valueless in themselves, merely serve as pretexts for his emotions. We can see in his narcissistic refusal of the loved one the intent to draw all his emotional faculties around him in order to adorn his own consciousness. Rather than the passion of consummated love which would fuse the lovers together, the young man prefers a calmer, almost sisterly affection in which, *à la Verlaine*, sensuality is tempered and redirected in a desire for consolation. He proposes to bypass entirely the first, passionate phase of love and to go directly to a later stage in which the weary disillusion of familiarity turns the lovers in upon themselves

---

[3] Paul Valéry, *Œuvres*, Gallimard, "Bibliothèque de la Pléiade," I, 126.

and upon their own past (p. 104). The young man even proposes that they love each other as if their affair were already a thing of the past; in this way they will be able to enhance that love in their imagination by evoking around it the illustrious examples of history and of their own fantasy.

> En sorte qu'aimant l'un et l'autre les plus parfaits des impossibles amants, nous croirons nous aimer nous-mêmes (p. 105).

As always with Barrès, the important thing is that the imagination be stimulated, that possession occur within the mind, and not that the affair at hand be led to a successful conclusion. This passage foreshadows the imaginative constructions that he builds around his selected "Objects" in the later books.

The fulfillment of desire in the past is a familiar romantic theme but, in this chapter and elsewhere in his early works, it is utilized for an analytic purpose. He is attempting to show symbolically that desire must be independent of its object if it is to survive. The possession of the desired object in the past, by memory, is an interiorization of desire. The object of desire is in fact the Self, of which the material object is only a pretext. The goal of *Le Culte du moi* is the possession of the Self and the analytic function of this episode is to lead to the conclusion: "nous croirons nous aimes nous-mêmes" (SB p. 105).

Passion, the single-minded projection of desire onto one object, is a possible means of achieving the unity of the Self, which is the spiritual goal of *Le Culte du moi*, but when desire is confused with its object the liberty and the very identity of the Self are threatened. The ideal solution is the conscious separation of desire and its object, by which the egotist can enjoy the intensity of passion without becoming its victim. He illustrates this idea ironically in Chapter Eleven of *Un Homme libre*, entitled "Une anecdote d'amour," in which Philippe sets out deliberately, in a controlled experiment, to enjoy all the emotions of a love affair with a girl whom he chooses at random. She is unintelligent and quite unworthy of his attention, with the result that his feelings are sure to be disassociated as far as possible from their object. Appropriately enough, he refers to her throughout as "l'Objet."

He treats love as a means of exercising the emotional faculties, as a kind of moral gymnastics, to use a term which he particularly liked. And when experienced as loss or absence, it can create that acuity of consciousness which is one of the fundamental goals of his egotism (the other being the possibility of creating around the chosen object an imaginative construction of ideas).

Now all of this is quite reminiscent of Des Esseintes' method in *A Rebours*. Huysmans' hero asserts that he has no need of the real world by shutting himself up in a house with the books, paintings, and other human artifacts which serve to stimulate his imagination. In order to savor the joys of a sea voyage, for example, he does not actually have to travel. It is sufficient for him to arrange one of his rooms to resemble the cabin of a ship. Philippe does not go this far, of course, but he is making the quite similar point that emotions can be manipulated independently of their object and that, for this reason, the object is to be considered as a creation of the imagination. The idea that emotion is more keenly experienced, more truly possessed in imagination goes back at least to Rousseau, but what Barrès seems to owe particularly to Huysmans is the methodical application of this insight to devalue objective experience in favor of subjective emotion. Huysmans, through the image of Des Esseintes' isolation in his "refined Thebaid," and Barrès, with the notion of the artificially created "universe," are both maintaining that the world can be possessed within the confines of the mind.[4]

The idea that in love there is no real communication with another being but only a projection of one's own desires is quite frequently encountered at the close of the century.[5] It is doubtless an expression of the more general tendency of sensibility in these years to feel that each man is walled up in his own mental universe. This is true of Proust's world to a very great extent. Although *A la recherche du temps perdu* did not begin to appear until 1913, the work has its roots in the same general period of

---

[4] Huysmans devalues experience, but he does not devalue objects themselves. Jewels, flowers, perfumes, rare books, etc. are the objects of Des Esseintes' predilection because of their *intrinsic* value. Clearly this aspect of Huysmans' imagination is quite foreign to Barrès.

[5] This theme is given strong expression, for instance, in Rémy de Gourmont's novel, *Sixtine* (1890).

the last twenty years of the 19th century. In particular, Proust's view of love is quite similar to that of Barrès when he describes the object of passion as a creation of our desire, quite unknowable in itself and distorted beyond recognition. We can perhaps see a further parallel in the way the analytic imagination is most active when the loved one is no longer present. The emotions of love for Proust are predominantly those of suffering in the absence of the loved one. Artistically and spiritually, love seems to fulfill a similar purpose in that it sets all the faculties in creative motion, even if this acuity is a source of pain. Indeed Proust's esthetic postulates suffering as the essential condition of artistic creation. Love is a much less central theme in Barrès' writing, but one can see a similar psychological view of experience in the works of the two men.

In downgrading the objective world in this way, Barrès is drawing a logical, if cynical, conclusion from his observation that his age was undermined by its sense of nihilism and relativity. In the *Dédicace* to *Un Homme libre,* he says that it is essential to convince oneself that there are only ways of seeing and no certainty (p. xviii). It is these "ways of seeing" that must be cultivated, as if they were absolute, but in the knowledge that they are only relative. "Les désirs, les ardeurs, les aspirations sont tout; le but rien" (HL. p. 236). The point that he is making is that the enthusiasm and the personal conviction which were directed towards the absolute must be retained even though one is convinced that there is no absolute. Later in his life, he was to use the expression "mes vérités" when referring to his doctrine. This linking of the plural and the possessive adjective is highly revealing of his attitude. Truth has been fragmented into innumerable subjective truths and the egotist cherishes those which he has shaped in his own image.

In *Un Homme libre,* however, Philippe is not holding defensively to a few selected ideas. On the contrary, he intends to experience as many different emotions as possible. Using a "mechanical method" he supplies his mind with powerful images which, interposed between the soul and the "ominous outside world," will allow him to enjoy "all the convictions, all the passions, and even the greatest exaltations that the human spirit is able to encounter" (H2 p. 39). Barrès' separation of the Self and the World permits a kind of neutralization of the latter. The objectively existing world is replaced by the "universe," a creation of his imaginative projections. The egotist is now in control; he is able to select as he will the objects of his emotion. The Universe is composed of nothing but what he has chosen, while at the same time he is free to choose everything.

A favorite idea in *Un Homme libre* is that the egotist can experience at will the whole range of ideas and feelings of which humanity is capable. It is in this sense that Philippe says that he and Simon are "reductions" (p. 39); they are able to contain in themselves the totality of the world. The egotist is seeking not only the ideal realization of the individual Self but the universality of all possible emotions which have been or could be known by all men: "Je paraîtrai devant moi-même comme la somme sans cesse croissante des sensations" (HL. p. 40). He even comes to say a little later that our soul and the universe are identical; they are both "the sum of all possible emotions" (HL. p. 65). The egotist has succeeded in eliminating the *différence* or otherness of the world. The universe is thus a reservoir of sensations for him; it is composed of the ideas, people, places, and things selected by himself and charged with his own emotion. The idea that all things are indifferent in themselves should lead to a quite arbitrary selection of objects for auto-stimulation and his ambition to experience all possible emotions should lead to a constant renewal. Nonetheless, although his theory of emotion denies any value to the non-Self, the fact remains that there are privileged objects in his universe. It is indeed highly selective. Lorraine, Venice, Toledo, Aigues-Mortes, Wagner, Disraeli, etc., occupy the space of his universe as sources of creative inspiration on the one hand and as imaginative reconstructions on the other.

III. *The Cult of the Self*

We have seen that the egotist's Narcissism brings him to an awareness of an inner Self beneath the troubled surface of consciousness, that part of the Self which is engaged in the flux of life. The inner Self is little more than the consciousness of consciousness at first, an awareness of an inner distance separating the most intimate part of himself from the succession of states which are the continuity of mental life. This distinction allows him to downgrade the contingent, existential Self which is a part of the world of transistory appearance.[6]

In the chapter "Extase," this is made quite explicit as the young man experiences a division of his consciousness. The detached, exalted, God-like self rises above his everyday Self and a dialogue develops in which the inner Self refuses to be discouraged by the "realistic" objections of the outer Self:

> —Mes pensées, mon âme, que m'importe! Je sais en quelle estime tenir ces représentations imparfaites de mon moi, ces images fragmentaires et furtives où vous prétendez me juger. Moi qui suis la loi des choses, et par qui elles existent dans leurs différences et dans leur unité, pouvez-vous croire que je me confonde avec mon corps, avec mes pensées, avec mes actes, toutes vapeurs grossières qui s'élèvent de vos sens quand vous me regardez! (pp. 239-240).

The inner Self is not to be confused with the content of consciousness, nor with what the person actually does, thinks, or says, nor even with his personality. This attitude, expressed here with the typical Barresian mixture of arrogance, naive candor, and abstraction, is very convenient for the egotist and is really quite central to Barrès' stance in the world. The devaluation of the existential personality allows him to bypass completely those empirical theories of the Self which would reduce it to the mere succession of its states and idea associations.[7] The essential being is placed out of reach of this kind of determinism.

---

[6] Thus the young man says to his mistress: "Vous daignez goûter quelques formes où j'habite et jamais vous n'atteindrez à m'aimer moi-même" (SB p. 101).

[7] Taine, for instance, attacked the idea of the *Idoélogue*, Maine de Biran, that there was an unchangeable Self to which passing sensations adhere (the "bâton d'ambre"). Taine refused to disassociate the Self from the sensations which constitute its consciousness: "En fait d'éléments réels et de matériaux positifs, je ne trouve donc, pour constituer mon être, que mes événements et mes états futurs, présents, passés. Ce qu'il y a d'effectif en moi, c'est leur série ou leur trame" (*De l'intelligence*, Livre III, 2ème Partie, "La Connaissance de l'esprit," p. 207. Quoted by Pierre Moreau, "Autour du culte du moi; essai sur les origines de l'égotisme français," *Archives des lettres modernes*, No. 7 [December, 1957], p. 6).

At this point, Barrès' thinking on the theme of inner freedom has led him to a position which is quite the opposite of Taine's and Zola's view of man as a social being determined by the circumstances of his heredity and environment. Taine and Zola both see man as a collective entity, whereas Barrès in *Le Culte du moi* is interested in the revolt of the individual against the society which has formed him. He cannot accept a point of view which would limit his freedom or render him psychologically dependent on his immediate environment. On the other hand, he eventually adopts a position which clearly bears the stamp of Taine's influence when he declares that the individual is the product of his ancestors. In attempting to understand this contradiction, one can say that his ideas in the first two volumes of the trilogy, in as much as they derive from an initial movement of revolt, have their own logic and take a direction quite different from the one Barrès was ultimately to follow. He himself argued that the affirmation of liberty is a necessary prelude to the acceptance of his determinism. While I would not wish to deny the truth of this chronological view of his thinking, I do not think that it fully accounts for the complexity of his position with regard to Taine. I am inclined to read *Le Culte du moi* as a dialectic of sensibility which is not just chronological but which exposes analytically the different moments of a complex attitude that, in its fundamental dynamics, is always characteristic of Barrès.

In the first place, he reduces Taine's three factors *race, milieu,* and *moment* to one. Only race remains as a significant determining factor [8] and here again we can see a singular limitation of Taine's ideas, because Barrès reduces race to the provincial or regional collectivity. His notion is really a mystique of being as authentic belonging rather than a critical instrument for examining different national cultures. Another difference — in my opinion the most important — is that Barrès affirms his "racial" origins in a spirit of opposition to the world in which he finds himself. His acceptance of his determinism is a means of negating the actual reality

---

[8] More precisely, it can be said that, by his doctrine of *La Terre et les Morts,* Barrès merges *race* and *milieu* into one single factor. However, the emphasis is on the hereditary transmission of essential being through the souls of the ancestors rather than on the influence of the living environment.

of modern France in the name of a deeper continuity. His authentic Self has to be discovered, unearthed as it were, from where it is hidden in the depths of his being. In the same way, Lorraine is not immediately accessible and certainly not to detached, critical analysis. Its secret must be penetrated by that mysterious communication between the sensibility of the observer and the profound spirit of the land which occurs in Barrès' meditations. Knowledge for him is not the objective accumulation and sorting of observable facts, but rather the fusing of two intimacies.

The distinction between the "real" Self deep inside one's being and the superficial Self which one shows to the outside world has the further advantage of placing the egotist out of reach of criticism. He can blandly disown his actions has he can even forestall the objections of his own reason and of his possible critics by speaking derogatively of his mediocrity, secure in the intimate conviction of his worth. The *dédoublement* we have observed is no doubt part of Barrès' romantic inheritance. It is the divided consciousness, the ironic inner distance common to so many writers in the 19th century, the source of a particular kind of lucidity and suffering, but also of their keen awareness of their uniqueness as infinitely valuable. Baudelaire's *conscience dans le mal* may be infernal, but it is his only guarantee of spirituality; it is his justification.

Barrès was, I think, faithful to this attitude all his life. He maintained that same ironic detachment in all his public posturing and political engagement, always leaving to the deepest part of himself the right to have the last word. He never allowed himself, in his own mind, to be committed or determined by his actions. How different is his position from that of the existentialists in this respect!

> Soyons convaincus que les actes n'ont aucune importance, car ils ne signifient nullement l'âme qui les a ordonnés et ne valent que par l'interprétation qu'elle leur donne (HL. p. 234),

and again:

> Se détacher de soi-même, chose belle et nécessaire! D'ailleurs, *mon moi du dehors,* que me fait! Les actes ne

comptent pas; ce qui importe uniquement, c'est mon *moi du dedans!* le Dieu que je construis (HL. p. 165).

Barrès appears in many ways as the exact opposite of Sartre who hated the memory of his own childhood and for whom the inner world of consciousness is abhorrent (the images of subjectivity in his works always translate a feeling of disgust). Escape for Sartre lies in the wholesomeness of active living, in reintegration into the virile community or ordinary men. Yet, like Barrès, Sartre seems to be seeking an authentic life and a lost identity, and, as is true of Barrès, the moment of rupture is situated in the past when the child discovered his loneliness and humiliation. Sartre would no doubt consider Barrès' alienation — his choice to live at a distance from himself and the world, and his project for self-reintegration — as a vast literary neurosis. But then it has its equivalent in the neurosis described in *Les Mots*.

However, it has already been noted that, although Barrès downgrades action and refuses to be defined by it, he does not preclude it. Indeed, the therapy of *Le Culte du moi* is designed to prepare the egotist for a new active contact with the world.[9] However, his insistence on the subjective value of action and his sense of detachment have the effect of reducing acts to gestures. The greatest act for Barrès is simply *to be* — provided that being is a testimony of integrity and authenticity. Thus être *soi-même*, être *lorrain*, and être *français* become highly meaningful acts in themselves. They have to the highest degree that quality of the act, which is to *appear* in the world, as manifestations, as visible achievements, and as operations capable of influencing the course of events.

He never felt himself completely involved in his various public acts, although, of course, he devoted so much of his time and energy to public life. His action in the *Assemblée*, the day to day political business of a *député*, his many speeches around the

---

[9] The desire for action and the question of commitment are the subject of *Toute licence sauf contre l'amour* which Barrès wrote in 1892 shortly after the completion of *Le Culte du moi* and in which he attempted to resolve the antinomy between thought and action in a period when national life had so little to offer the enthusiasms of young men.

country, and his tireless propaganda for the French Army during the war were, from the point of view of the detached literary self, non-essential, merely expressions of energy and a need for commitment. The writer always remained at a painful distance from the active self. Thus it is that while he was deeply rooted in a certain historical moment he appeared at the same time a solitary, aloof, and original figure, oddly detached from the world and from himself.

The ideal Self is quite a vague notion at first in *Le Culte du moi;* it is merely the unknown goal of his aspiration. In trying to describe what he means, Barrès uses exalted expressions like "the sum of all possible emotions," and he goes on to link this idea to God. Thus God is defined as "la somme des émotions ayant conscience d'elles-mêmes" (HL. p. 121). Characteristically, the realization of the ideal requires a kind of infinite expansion of the powers of feeling to embrace the entire world. There is probably an echo of Hartmann's philosophy in the idea of a passage from unconscious to conscious existence, particularly noticeable in a text like the following:

> J'entrevis que l'effort de tous mes instincts aboutissait à la pleine conscience de moi-même, et qu'ainsi je deviendrais Dieu, si un temps infini était donné à mon être (HL. p. 193).

His project, then, is to cultivate in himself a state of perpetual ardor, and the object of this vital impulse he calls God.[10]

---

[10] Renan's influence is discernable in Barrès' conception of the Ideal as a God to be created. For the historian, "God" is the end of the process of historical *fieri:*

> L'idéal existe; il est éternel; mais il n'est pas encore matériellement réalisé; il le sera un jour. Il sera réalisé par une conscience analogue à celle de l'humanité, mais infiniment supérieure, laquelle, comparée à notre état présent, si horrible, si chétif, semblera une parfaite machine à vapeur auprès de la vieille machine de Marly. L'œuvre universelle de tout ce qui vit est de faire Dieu parfait, de contribuer à la grande résultante définitive qui clora le cercle des choses par l'unité (*Dialogues philosophiques*, II, *Œuvres complètes*, I, 597).

This last sentence, only slightly different in wording, occurs also in *L'Avenir de la science, Œuvres complètes*, III, 757.

Religion is the central image in *Un Homme libre* and must be related to the very title of the trilogy: *Le Culte du moi*. Already in *Sous l'œil des barbares,* the use of the religious analogy was apparent,[11] but the imagery in *Un Homme libre* goes beyond the imprecise religious atmosphere of the earlier novel. The cult is now a specifically Catholic one. A glance at the table of contents is sufficient to show to what an extent the analogy of egotism with Catholic faith is central to the composition of the novel. The first three parts are entitled "En état de grâce," "L'Église militante," and "L'Église triomphante" and the chapter headings also suggest the organization of a spiritual manual. The rhythm of the book is that of a spiritual ascension towards the fortification of faith by meditation and ascesis.

The sojourn of Philippe and Simon in Lorraine is explicitly a religious retreat, inspired by the *Imitation of Christ* (Book I, chapter XX, "On the Love of Solitude and of Silence"). The spiritual quest for an absolute egotism parallels the attainment of sainthood. First there is desire, the state of grace in which the egotist longs for union with God. Then follows the period of struggle in which he searches for the psychological ground of faith, methodically analyzing the conditions for ecstasy. And finally there is the triumph of faith, when the egotist enters into his paradise of permanent emotion, in perfect control of his capacity for feeling. The kingdom of heaven (Mon royaume n'est pas de ce monde..." (HL. p. 165) is thus an image of the "universe." Philippe's quest is accompanied by prayer, confession, spiritual meditation, and ascetic discipline. The method which he applies in his meditations is specifically an adaptation of Loyola's psychological technique in the *Spiritual Exercises*. The categories of religion are carried over to the perfection of egotism; even the notion of sin has its equivalent — in everything that is tepid, gray, lacking in fever, everything that is destructive of enthusiasm (HL. p. 165).

The appropriateness of religion as an image of the cult of the Self is that, for Barrès, the desire for emotional intensity is exactly equivalent to religious feeling. Faith, for him, is essentially an

---

[11] J'avais hâte de cette nuit, ô mon bien-aimé, ô moi, pour redevenir un dieu" (SB, p. 238).

exalted feeling beyond the normal, down-to-earth functioning of the heart and mind. Its particularity is its capacity to bridge the gap between desire and its attainment, and to lift the individual beyond the limits of his individuality rooted in space and time. What attracts Barrès in the religious experience is not its rational basis as belief and intellectual conviction, but rather the quality of the experience itself. In accordance with one of the principal tenets of his egotism, that it is the quality of the emotion alone that counts, he values the desire for God because of the intensity of the longing.

In the religious experience, Barrès particularly values its current of mysticism,[12] that irrational urge which raises a man beyond the "real" world to an ecstatic union of the Self and a higher reality. He is drawn to the exhilarating spiritual heroism of the saints and martyrs, for, in the terms of his imagination, their sufferings are noble and their distinction from the ordinary run of men magnificent. Their single-minded pursuit of an absolute ideal is a surpassing of the bounds of normal human capacity for feeling. Similarly, he is drawn to the vision of the solitary man in his cell,[13] imagining his life in the bare, austere surroundings as a continual overheating of the imagination, a feverish, anguished, and sometimes glorious exaltation.

So Philippe and Simon are delighted to find an old cloister in the property which they rent in Lorraine for their monkish retreat. The pursuit of liberty is comparable to that of the Christian mystic who is freed from the enslavement to his temporal self and who is the absolute master of his own physiological mechanism. The egotists find that the Catholic cult corresponds not only to their ardent desire for self-possession and spiritual fulfillment, but also to their need for a restraining discipline. The search for authenticity on which to ground emotion entails a

---

[12] Mme Frandon defines Barrès' conception of the mystical state as the linking of a religious and a poetic state (*L'Orient de Maurice Barrès*, p. 228).

[13] Jacques Vier notes that the theme of the cell was common towards the end of the century and he traces its origin to Huysmans' *A rebours*: "Premier effort de réaction contre les Barbares, première hantise de la cellule, tentative curieuse de sécularisation de l'ascétisme, découverte laborieuse de tremplins nouveaux pour l'essor des rêves" ("Barrès et le culte du moi," p. 10).

certain *dépouillement,* a certain intellectual and physical austerity. Philippe's room at Saint-Germain is a cell for him; the empty walls are the analogy not only of his spiritual detachment, but also, by the absence of anything which would attach him to the past, of the soul's constantly renewed liberty (HL. p. 30). To complete the illusion, the two young men impose on their lives a monastic rule, remaining silent until the hour of the evening meal, organizing their activities on a fixed schedule, and conducting their meditations systematically.

Barrès' debt to the Baudelaire of the *Journaux intimes* in this view of religion must be emphasized.[14] The opening sentence of *Fusées* might well serve to set the tone for *Un Homme libre:* "Quand même Dieu n'existerait pas, la Religion serait encore Sainte et *Divine.*"[15] It was Baudelaire who introduced Barrès to

---

[14] See Mme Frandon, *L'Orient,* p. 364 and note 1, pp. 448-49: "Que d'expressions, ou d'attitudes de pensée qui des *Journaux intimes* sont passées chez Barrès! Notons par exemple, l'emploi de mots du vocabulaire des religions ('saint,' 'salut') détachés de toute valeur religieuse précise, bien qu'ils conservent sans doute une résonance religieuse."

See also Mme Goosse, "A propos de *Sous l'œil des barbares*" and P.-G. Castex, "Aux sources d'*Un Homme libre,*" *Revue d'histoire littéraire de la France,* 59 (January-March, 1959), 71-86. M. Castex, who has examined the manuscript of *Un Homme libre,* reveals that Barrès had planned to include Baudelaire as the third "intercessor" after Benjamin Constant and Sainte-Beuve. He shows that, although Barrès suppressed this section so as not to make the chapter too long, the influence of Baudelaire is manifest throughout the book. The terms *bohémianisme, intercesseur,* and *acédia,* used by Barrès, were taken from the poet's reflections in the *Journaux intimes* (pp. 78-79). He points out (p. 77) that the quotation at the end of Philippe's meditation on Sainte-Beuve ("Avant tout, être un grand homme et un saint pour soi-même" [HL, p. 91]) is from *Mon Cœur mis à nu* (*Œuvres complètes,* p. 1289).

Barrès may well have been inspired by Baudelaire in his choice of the title of the trilogy. In *Fusées,* one of the brief notations in large type is "Auto-idolâtrie" (*Œuvres complètes,* p. 1256), and, of course, dandyism is a cult of the Self. Also in *Fusées,* Baudelaire writes: "Du culte de soi-même dans l'amour, au point de vue de la santé, de l'hygiène, de la toilette, de la noblesse spirituelle et de l'éloquence" (p. 1257). One can in fact trace most of the principal themes of *Un Homme libre* to the *Journaux intimes:* the idea of religion, sainthood, prayer, methodical self-perfection, accompanied by measures of physical and mental hygiene. The tone and the meaning given to these themes are, however, quite different in Barrès' work and, in noting certain parallels, we should not forget the originality of *Le Culte du moi,* an originality which consists precisely in a certain way of appropriating the lessons of his elders.

[15] *Œuvres complètes,* p. 1247.

the idea that the value and beauty of religion were not in the God it served, but in the forms of the cult itself; that its vocabulary was appropriate, not because of the objective supernatural truth conveyed, but because of its psychological truth; and that the specific value of Catholicism was its extraordinary power as a psychological mechanism for the stimulation of the imagination and the deepening of the sense of existence.

Barrès' cult of the Self is founded, then, on a double conceit. It is an appropriation of both the language of religion and a certain philosophical discourse on the nature of the ego. It was fashionable in the period when he wrote *Le Culte du moi* to give a poetico-philosophical seriousness to literary works. This was the age of Symbolism when mysticism and metaphysics were cultivated as a means of escaping from the hated reality of existence. And also at this time, there was a marked tendency to adapt what properly belongs to the religious sensibility to esthetic and psychological ends, as the works of Baudelaire, Huysmans, and the Symbolists amply demonstrate. The success of the trilogy was due in no small degree to its "metaphysical" treatment of the popular theme of the solitary individual who denies the reality of the world because he feels estranged from it.

As for the role of this metaphysical dimension in his works, two remarks are in order. First of all, if the metaphysics of the Self seem rather puerile, this is deliberately so, because Barrès is evidently turning the adolescent's enthusiasm for abstract ideas into a weapon to be used against his spiritual oppressors. There is an element of irony and defiance in the way he appropriates the lessons of his intellectual mentors and diverts them from their intended context to suit his own self-affirmation. He is throwing what he has learned at school back in the faces of his masters. Nonetheless, it remains true that Barrès is always searching for something solid on which to ground his ideas, and he has a noticeable liking for formulae, abstractions, and analytic systems. The philosophical dimension enables him to give a framework to his reflections.

In the case of his metaphorical use of religious vocabulary, Barrès' irony reaches lyrical heights, so much that the unwary reader might take him entirely seriously and wonder how he could ever have adopted such an inflated tone. Nowhere in *Le Culte du moi* do we feel more intensely the calculated exaggeration and iconoclastic brashness of the young intellectual dandy than in certain passages of *Un Homme libre*. However, it is also evident that his design is basically serious. In all his works, he makes use of the psychological and liturgical structures of religion to organize his spiritual meditations. Yet there is a great difference between the texts of these early novels and his later works in which the irony and the metaphorical thrust have given way to a more literal religiosity. The "ideology" of the trilogy is fictionalized and poetized and cannot be read as a straightforward analytic text in which Philippe is "merely" the mouthpiece of his creator. In *Un Homme libre,* the religious analogy plays an important role in removing the text from the psychological *reality* of Barrès' own experience.

IV. *Liberty and Identity*

I have already alluded to the fact that Barrès' thought seems to develop in two quite different directions in *Un Homme libre*. The affirmation of absolute liberty is not altogether compatible with the other principal idea of the novel that the egotist must recognize his racial determinism. The impulse to Godlike self-realization aims at a total possession of the world and a complete rejection of any constraint. These are the two conditions of absolute freedom. This means that the egotist must maintain his enthusiasm at a constantly high pitch, always ready to experience a new sensation, while remaining free of all attachments. It requires a state of *disponibilité* and *dénuement* which foreshadows Gide.

> Je vais jusqu'à penser que ce serait un bon système de vie de n'avoir pas de domicile, d'habiter n'importe où dans le monde. Un chez moi est un prolongement du passé; les émotions d'hier le tapissent. Mais coupant sans cesse derrière moi, je veux que chaque matin la vie m'apparaisse neuve, et que toutes choses me soient un début (HL. p. 237).

Clearly *Un Homme libre* is at the origin of the ethic which Gide elaborates in *Les Nourritures terrestres*.[16] There are many pas-

---

[16] Aragon underlines Gide's debt to Barrès and castigates him for his

sages, like the one I have just quoted, that could be transposed directly into Gide's work. Is there any more "Gidian" axiom than this, for example? "Nulle fièvre ne me demeurera inconnue et nulle ne me fixera" (HL. p. 40).

Gide develops Barrès' themes in quite a different direction, and far beyond anything his predecessor could accept — in a sense, *Les Nourritures terrestres* begins where *Un Homme libre* ends — but the similarities are striking on a number of points. Gide continues Barrès' analysis of desire, and like his elder he separates desire from its object ("Que l'*importance* soit dans ton regard, non dans la chose regardée") [17] in order to cultivate the purity of ardor. Both men use the idea of God to translate this ideal direction of their longing ("Comprends qu'à chaque instant du jour tu peux posséder Dieu dans sa totalité"). [18] Gide's ethic is also directed towards self-perfection and total possession of the universe, and he insists like Barrès that the world can be possessed in the mind through the imaginative understanding: "Comprendre, c'est se sentir capable de faire. ASSUMER LE PLUS POSSIBLE D'HUMANITÉ, voilà la bonne formule." [19] Not only do we recognize here Barrès' ambition to expand his individual consciousness to a universal potentiality for experience, but we also find the same use of the axiom, echoing Philippe's "Sentir le plus possible."

Gide's debt to Barrès goes beyond this kind of obvious borrowing of themes, however. The ethic expressed in *Les Nourritures terrestres* is only one of several tendencies which coexisted in the young Gide, and his sensibility has its own complexities which are quite different from Barrès'. The principal lesson which Gide learned from him was that it was possible to create a literature, at once lyrical and ethical in tone, based upon the dialectics of sensibility in its confrontation with its own desires and the world in which it finds itself. Gide probably went further in transform-

---

betrayal of his master: "La critique sans mesure de Barrès n'a fait place nette qu'au Nathanaël des *Nourritures terrestres,* que Gide n'aurait jamais enfanté tout seul, et qui a vilainement renié ce qu'il devait à son véritable père" ("En guise de préface," in *L'Œuvre de Maurice Barrès,* Vol. II, xii-xiii).

[17] André Gide, *Romans, récits et soties. Œuvres lyriques,* Gallimard, Bibliothèque de la Pléiade, 1958, p. 155.
[18] Ibid., p. 162.
[19] Ibid., p. 158.

ing the multiplicity of the world into inner richness and diversity. He realized more successfully a certain tendency of the Barresian ideal by virtue of his peculiar qualities of curiosity, sympathy, comic sense, and openness of mind, together with his greater ability to project himself into fictional creations that are *possible* developments of the different Selves within him.

Thus the logic of Barrès' revolt carries him to an extreme position which Gide was to adopt in his equally extreme manual of revolt and freedom. Freedom is a delivrance from the prison of family, upbringing, and society and it is an escape from the slavery of the superficial personality. The result of such a radical break with the continuity of life is to plunge the individual out of time into a vertiginous present. He is cut off from his past and unable to construct a future. More than Barrès, Gide analyzes the dangers of such a position, in *Les Nourritures terrestres* and then in *L'Immoraliste*. For a moment, Philippe seems to experience something of this vertigo, as he tells Simon in a letter which sums up the results of his experiments at the end of the book:

> Étranger au monde extérieur, étranger même à mon passé, étranger à mes instincts, connaissant seulement des émotions rapides que j'aurai choisies: véritablement Homme libre" (pp. 239-240).[20]

Philippe feels that he is detached even from his instincts, whereas the Immoralist has the impression of rediscovering a deeper, more authentic, more powerful Self underneath the veneer of the civilized man when he learns how to release his instinctual desires. In the case of Gide, the anarchical impulse of instinct is a primary liberating value. In *Un Homme libre* the extreme of liberty is a dizzy sensation of oneself as a complete abstraction and as an

---

[20] Jean Duvignaud, in his article "Barrès l'étranger," calls him a classic example of the "anomic personality," profoundly unadapted to society by virtue of his vocation as a writer. He considers that the "étrangeté" of Barrès was a permanent feature of his relationship with the world, the measure of the "distance" which separated him from it: "Parce que son discours poétique l'éloigne de lui-même, il tente de renouer avec des 'vertus' qui l'attachent à des valeurs fixes.... Si bien que l'on devrait regarder l'œuvre de Barrès comme un long effort, répété sur des registres divers, pour compenser une solitude permanente, une étrangeté profondément vécue mais jamais avouée. Et cela jusqu'au dernier jour" (p. 496).

entirely artificial creation. For Barrès, liberty in itself does not lead to authenticity, although, as we shall see, it is the necessary prelude to its discovery.

This second novel of the trilogy ends on a note of discouragement. Philippe is in a typically Barresian state of nervous crispation, so that he is capable only of negating. He has learned much about himself, and no doubt he feels in control of his own psychic mechanism, but he does not know how to use the machine which he has perfected. In this same letter to Simon, we find him enumerating the possible developments he might have given to his talents and rejecting them all. He might have been a "marvellous instrument for producing rare phenomena" or he could have cultivated a delicate neurosis and complained about his inability to live (pp. 236-37). He concludes the list with the exclamation: "May my natural virtues remain within me a closed, uncultivated garden." (p. 237). By the dynamics of the impulse towards absolute freedom, Philippe reaches a position which is diametrically opposed to the one with which Barrès is usually associated and which in fact Philippe himself adopts in *Le Jardin de Bérénice*, where the cultivation of natural virtue is one of the main themes. However, the thrust of this text is that the egotist will not yield to a "natural" penchant which might have made of him a Decadent and a dilettante *à la* des Esseintes. He has been saved from taking up any banal attitude characteristic of his contemporaries by the very excess of his "artificial" method which has completely cut him away from all facile tendencies.

Parallel to this drive which tends to *depersonalize* the Self, to divest it of all its affective links with the world, and to transform it into a mere aptitude for experiencing the universality of emotion, there is another impulse at work towards identity and identification. The egotist has discovered that his ideal is to bring to consciousness the greatest possible number of experiences in order to enjoy a boundless feeling of possession. Now, in the chapter devoted to his sojourn in Lorraine, this idea becomes inflected towards something quite different. There is a temptation to limit the expansion of the individual Self to the idea that the egotist will bring to consciousness in his mind the spirit of the collectivity to which he belongs. The soul of Lorraine speaks to him in the course of his meditation, explaining that the collective soul realizes itself more or less perfectly in the individual whose role is to bring into maximum consciousness the potentialities of the race.[21] What is required now is no longer detachment, but identification with something outside the Self. The change of orientation in his thought occurs around the idea of instinct and the unconscious, which Barrès tends more and more to associate with a transpersonal collective life accessible to the individual as a continuation of his own limited existence. The point of access to the racial unconscious is through the deepest instincts which constitute the authentic being of the individual. The inner Self is no longer conceived as a mere function, but as an identity which can be revealed. So the quest for self-knowledge takes a different direction now.

We can follow this quest in a complex of metaphorical and thematic developments by which Barrès literalizes, or concretizes, the inner space of the Self in its two principal dimensions: horizontal and vertical. The exploration of the Self is likened to the drawing up of a map which would demarcate his character. He uses the term "moral geography" to convey this idea.[22] The content of consciousness, the inner distance within the mind, is materialized as a land which can be explored. Its limits are often evoked by the image of the horizon which gives an idea of extension, reflecting the dilation of the Self in its expansive desire.

> Cependant une fois encore, dans cette atmosphère de son Moi, là-bas sur l'horizon de cet univers volontaire qui

---

[21] "C'est peut-être en ton âme que moi, Lorraine, je me serai connue le plus complètement. Mais ce futur, qui est en elle [ta race] à l'état de désir et qu'elle n'a plus l'énergie de réaliser, cultive-le prends-en une idée claire" (HL p. 131).

[22] Already at the time of *Les Taches d'encre*, Barrès had used this image: "Je dirai les systèmes modernes, de leur orient à leur couchant, à travers les âmes sœurs. Et il me plairait d'indiquer d'un trait sobre leurs frontières, pour les situer dans la carte du monde moral contemporain" (*Les Taches d'encre*, p. 389). And reflecting upon the advice of M. X..., the young man objects: "Il bornait mon horizon à ces apparences que, pour la facilité des relations mondaines ou commerciales, tous les Parisiens admettent, et dont les journaux à quinze centimes vous tracent chaque matin la géographie" (SB p. 209). In *Le Jardin de Bérénice*, Philippe says of his friend: "Simon a véritablement le sens de la géographie des âmes; il sait dans quelle région intellectuelle je suis situé" (p. 119).

n'est que son âme déroulée à l'infini, il devine la jeune femme (SB. pp. 232-33).

The phrase "son âme déroulée à l'infini" admirably evokes Barrès' ideal of self-contemplation. Sometimes, however, the feeling of sterility reduces this horizon to a dreary space, a worthless terrain like a riding-track trodden up by the same worn-out feelings (SB. p. 171).

The images of the geography and the horizon of the Self tend to give a more concrete, more literal meaning to the notion of the "universe." It is materialized as the surface extension of the egotist's capacity for emotion, the limits of his attitudes, thoughts, and feelings. Within the inner space of his mind, there is, then, a horizontal plane constituted by what is compatible with his soul.

> J'avais là, campés devant moi comme une carte de géographie, tous les points que, grâce à mon analyse, j'ai relevés et décrits en mon âme:
> D'abord un vaste territoire, mon tempérament, produisant avec abondance une belle variété de phénomènes, rebelles à certaines cultures, stérile sur plusieurs points, où des parties sont encore à découvrir, pâles, indécises et flottantes (HL. pp. 126-27).

However, the exploration of the Self is also conducted vertically as he uncovers the successive layers which constitute the geological strata of his being. *Sous l'œil des barbares* was more concerned with tracing the geography of the Self in its relation with the outside world in order to establish the existence of a specific domain which was *himself*. *Un Homme libre* explores his "universe" in depth.

The idea of a descent into the Self in order to dig out its authenticity is already presented towards the end of *Sous l'œil des barbares:* "Je m'en tiens à dégager mon Moi des alluvions qu'y rejette sans cesse le fleuve immonde des Barbares" (p. 241). The geological term "alluvions" concretizes the idea that the real Self must be unearthed (the key word here is *dégager*) from beneath everything that is non-essential and foreign. So after the unhappy experiences among the Barbarians, the young man will appear *fouillé* and *aminci* (SB. p. 266) as he sets out to explore his own being. The word *couches* is used throughout *Un Homme libre* to describe the geological strata within the Self. The intercessors, Benjamin Constant and Sainte-Beuve, represent two levels of Philippe's sensibility. By meditating upon them, he discovers some of his deepest tendencies reflected in their attitudes and reaction to life. However, they do not represent the bedrock of his authenticity:

> Mais j'entrevois que ces couches superposées de ma conscience, à qui je donne les noms d'hommes fameux, ne sont pas du tout mon Moi (HL. p. 92).

He speculates that perhaps they only illustrate the most recent parts of his consciousness. The spatial dimension of the geological strata is the image of a temporal conception of the formation of the Self. Farthest back in time is the racial consciousness, beyond the limits of the individual's own experience but nevertheless an integral part of the Self. Following the meditations upon his intercessors, Philippe examines the history of Lorraine, and in one of the aspects of his temperament — his melancholy — he recognizes the legacy of the past:

> Dans mon patrimoine de mélancolie, il reste quelque parcelle des inquiétudes que mes ancêtres ont ressenties dans cet horizon.
>
> A suivre comme ils ont bâti leur pays, je retrouverai l'ordre suivant lequel furent posées mes propres assises. C'est une bonne méthode pour descendre dans quelques parties obscures de ma conscience (p. 93).

The idea that the cult of the Self is a descent into the underlying reality of consciousness is clearly expressed in this passage. This time, the spatial conception is illustrated by the image of the Self as an edifice. *Parcelle* is one of Barrès' favorite words, which he uses to denote blocks of emotional experience — and always with a very positive, spiritualized meaning. *Parcelle* can be translated as "part," "portion," but also as "a piece of land."

His emotional "universe" is composed first of all of the "geographical" projection of his character which constitutes the "first Self" (p. 127). Beyond that first Self, he distinguishes the figures of his intercessors, the next level of his authenticity, and beyond them, his ancestors. Two methods of self-development or "cultivation" are open to the egotist. He can continue the horizontal expansion of the Self; in this direction, he can satisfy his urge for constantly renewed emotion and for omnipotence. But the price to be paid for these exaltations is a feeling of extreme artificiality and of rootless detachment from himself and the world. Or he can carry out a vertical exploration towards the inner depths of his being, where he will hope to find authenticity, continuity, and identity. Certainly, Barrès opted for the second of these forms of self cultivation, but he never entirely renounced the other ambition of the free man.

CHAPTER III

THE BODY

What value should be attributed to the body in *Le Culte du moi?* The insistence on the superiority of instinct over intelligence might lead one to expect some glorification of it; but Barrès is no D. H. Lawrence, praising the fullness of life in the surge of the blood or seeking authenticity in genital activity and virile strength. On the contrary, the body is a puny thing, sickly and unexercised, as we might expect of a young man who had spent his life among his books or in the cafés of the city. The intelligence has been developed at the expense of the physical functions and, far from glorifying the body, Barrès treats it with a self-deprecatory irony, dwelling on its puniness and calling attention to the ills that beset it. In *Sous l'œil des barbares,* he exclaims almost derisively, "Qu'importe mon corps!" (p. 238). He dismisses it as a mere "plaything," infinitely inferior to that inner Self which is the object of his cult. He his in no way responsible for this "mediocre product" with which he was supplied at birth (p. 239). However, his attitude is not simply one of contempt for the body, for it is not altogether dismissed as an unworthy material receptacle for the mind it sustains. Certainly it is not a case of stoic disregard for the physical element of existence.

Barrès is one of many writers in the second half of the 19th Century who reflect in different ways a general preoccupation with psycho-physiological thinking. The passages in *Sous l'œil des barbares* and *Un Homme libre* which refer to the body and its functions have to be read in the context of the physiological realism which had been in vogue during the naturalist years if their full "ideological" and ironic force is to be felt. Barrès takes full advantage of the fact that his subject (the relation of the Self to the World) is a crossroads at which not only philosophy, but also its related discipline, psychology, converge on certain themes of current sensibility. In the latter part of the 19th Century, men were quite accustomed to a mixture of philosophical and psychological speculation, and he was able to make use at one and the same time of a somewhat transcendental, idealist way of talking about the Self and a view of the human being as a psycho-physiological mechanism. Idealism and materialism are strangely mixed in *Le Culte du moi*.

In its thinking about the nature of psychic phenomena, positive science in the 19th century developed the materialist orientation of 18th century philosophy. That is to say, there was a tendency to view mental phenomena as an extension of physiology and to reduce psychic activity to manifestations of organic conditions. As is well known, this had important repercussions in literature when the Goncourts and Zola turned to medical science for an explanation of individual behavior in society. There was a considerable downgrading of "psychology" in the presentation of character, motivation, and social destiny. Taine's provocative statement, echoed by Zola, that vice and virtue were products like suger and vitriol was characteristic of the impact of these ideas among laymen. The Goncourts developed a rather specialized fascination with pathological cases which lent themselves dramatically to their vision of socio-psychological disorder. The preponderance accorded to hereditary factors and fundamental behavioral disturbances on the one hand and to the Tainian theory of the influence of the social environment on the other reinforced a penchant, already discernable in realism, to consider human destinies as materially determined.

In a typically ironic and high-handed manner, Barrès reverses this whole way of thinking in one simple stroke. And he does this without attempting to refute the current ideas on psychology or to reaffirm idealistic notions of the independence of the human personality. He is quite prepared to see the body and its psychic adjunct, the soul, as a mechanical system, but he certainly does not intend to be determined by it. On the contrary, he turns this physiological reduction of the personality to his own advantage in asserting his principles of total freedom and self-creation. Since the physical constitution and the complex of impulses and feelings which derive from it produce mechanical responses to the situations in which the individual finds himsef, then it is up to the individual to take over conscious control of his own mechanism. Having established a fundamental discontinuity between the inner Self (the seat of consciousness and will) and the material, existential Self, the egotist is in a position to manipulate and direct the functioning of the machine by careful selection and dosing of the stimuli.

It is to religious psychology that he turns for a model upon which to base this method. The spiritual exercises of Loyola, which are designed to stimulate and direct the imaginative process around the object of their choice, provide him with a perfect analogy for his constructive meditations. Thus, in his determination to appropriate any idea that can serve his purpose, Barrès brings about a curious convergence of religious and positive psychology upon the idea that psychic processes are mechanical and that they can be manipulated.[1] In a sense which is quite different from what the naturalists understood by the term, but with its roots in the same pseudo-medical view of human behavior, *Un Homme libre* can be said to be an "experimental" novel. Once again, then, we see that his egotism is a carefully calculated mixture of sabotage and assimilation in which irony goes hand in hand with high adolescent seriousness.

Philippe's objective in *Un homme libre* is to perfect his "mechanical method" (p. 39) so as to generate emotional enthusiasm whenever he wishes — *à volonté* ("at will") is a frequent expression in the book. Thus he will become an "admirable machine" (p. 38); his soul will be a mechanical organ[2] which will play him

---

[1] Philippe remarks, for example, as he assesses the givens of his sensibility: "J'offre un phénomène bien connu des philosophes de la médecine et des directeurs de conscience: je passe par des alternatives incessantes de langueur et d'exaltation. C'est ainsi que je fus poussé à cette série d'expériences, où je veux me créer une exaltation continue et proscrire à jamais les abattements (HL p. 46).

[2] The choice of this particular image and the dilettantism which it reveals suggest a parallel with Des Esseintes' *orgue à bouche* in *A rebours*. (See Jacques Vier, "Barrès et le culte du moi," p. 10 and note 29, p. 57.) Barrès, taking his cue from Huysmans and Baudelaire, exalts artificiality

the most varied tunes when he presses the appropriate button (pp. 229-30); and he will be able to hold his "mechanized soul" in his hands ready to provide the rarest emotions (p. 62). He describes himself holding his soul in hand like a horse on a rein:

> On connaît ma méthode: je tiens en main mon âme pour qu'elle ne butte pas, comme un vieux cheval qui sommeille en trottant, et je m'ingénie à lui procurer chaque jour de nouveaux frissons. On m'accordera que j'excelle à la ramener dès qu'elle se dérobe (p. 233).

The image is ironically self-deprecatory. There is a deliberate deflating contrast between the decadent overrefinement of the "nouveau frisson" and the vision of the old horse.

Barrès' view of emotion as something mechanically generated serves as a means of undercutting his flights of romantic sensibility, of bringing himself down to earth, and of reminding himself of the modest, even mediocre foundations upon which his sentimental "universe" is built. But he is not just proposing a therapy for the Romantic Agony; his purpose is to transform romantic enthusiasm into a manageable source of spiritual energy. And, of course, it is also true that the more Philippe belittles his material Self through this kind of reduction, the more he exalts the godlike independence of his will.

Philippe's program, therefore, demands a knowledge of the laws by which his mental processes are governed. The psychological method of Loyola teaches him how to cultivate his emotions mechanically, but it is to Georges Cabanis that he turns for a physiological understanding of his temperament. In his *Rapports du physique et du moral de l'homme,* Cabanis had set out to demonstrate the dependence of mental activity upon the functioning of the other organs of the body. He shows that the brain is merely an organ among others and governed by the same laws of interdependence and reciprocal influence that can be observed in the lesser organs.[3] The moral personality is a mechanism, de-

---

in his early works, but he uses the term to describe the superior dilettantism of his emotional quest. He is concerned with artificial attitudes rather than with artificial stimuli.

[3] *Rapports du physique et du moral* in *Œuvres philosophiques,* Presses universitaires de France, 1956, Vol. I, 603.

termined by the interaction of the organs of the body and the reactions of these organs to the sensations which affect them. Thus ideas, instinctive inclinations, conscious desires, and affections: everything which constitutes the individual character, are mechanically produced.[4] This devaluation of the personality in Cabanis' system was in complete accord with Barrès' own idea that individual character is an accidental phenomenon quite different from the deep Self. He also finds support in Cabanis' work for his belief that it is possible to control the functioning of this mechanism. He concludes that a little practice should enable the egotist to generate the "rarest states of the human soul," (HL p. 38), simply by applying some vigorous hygienic and pharmaceutical measures.

Another similarity in the ideas of the two men is their interpretation of the Self. For Cabanis, as for Destutt de Tracy, the Self resides not in the personality but in the will,[5] and the will is the manifestation of the unique principle of the universe, of that primary force which he calls "spontaneity":

> Cette force n'est autre chose que le principe général du mouvement, la puissance active.... Je l'appelle spontanée, non que je prétende exprimer par là sa nature, mais parce que ce mot me paraît rendre l'impression qu'en reçoit l'intelligence bornée de l'homme, en voyant cette force agir sans relâche, avec une activité toujours nouvelle.[6]

---

[4] "Nous nous sommes assurés également, par des analyses réitérées, que les idées, les penchants instinctifs, les volontés raisonnées, et toutes les affections quelconques se forment par un mécanisme, parfaitement analogue à celui qui détermine les opérations et les mouvements organiques les plus simples; et que si le système cérébral, instrument direct de ces opérations plus relevées, exerce une grande action sur les systèmes vivants d'un ordre inférieur, cette action se rapporte entièrement, et par ses causes, et par la manière dont elle est produite, à celle qu'ils exercent les uns sur les autres, et dont lui-même il n'est point affranchi" (*Rapports*, pp. 605-606).

[5] Cabanis refers to Destutt de Tracy and summarizes his theory of the Self as awareness of Will: "Qu'en conséquence, l'impression, ou la conscience du *moi* senti, du *moi*, reconnu distinct des autres existences, ne peut s'acquérir que par la conscience d'un effort voulu; qu'en un mot, le *moi* réside exclusivement dans la volonté" (*Rapports*, p. 546).

[6] *Degré de certitude de la médecine*, p. 58.

Cabanis thought that it was impossible to know this force in its essence but that it could be apprehended in its effects in the phenomenal world. It is through his will that man participates directly in this universal force.[7]

The belief that the activity of the brain was a mechanical function like that of any other organ of the body led, of course, to a downgrading of intelligence, and in this Barrès is representative of a marked tendency among his contemporaries. Jules Soury, whom he knew personally, held views about the brain and the nature of intelligence which were very much a continuation of Cabanis' approach to psychology.[8] Psychic activity was rigorously determined by the physical mechanism of the organs,[9] the intelligence was functional, and consciousness was to be seen not so much as a spiritual entity as an effect, an epiphenomenon.[10]

---

[7] The parallels between these ideas and those of Schopenhauer and his disciple, Hartmann, are clear and may help to explain a remark Barrès makes in the Examen when he is discussing the Unconscious in *Le Jardin de Bérénice:* "De là ce troisième volume, *Le Jardin de Bérénice,* une théorie de l'amour, où les producteurs français qui tapageaient contre Schopenhauer et ne savaient reconnaître en lui l'esprit de notre dix-huitième siècle, pourront varier leurs développements, s'ils distinguent qu'ici l'on a mis Hartmann en action" (*Examen,* p. 28).

[8] "La psychologie, la science des fonctions psychiques de la matière vivante, depuis celles du protoplasma indifférencié de certains protozoaires jusqu'aux plus hautes activités du système nerveux de l'homme, n'est donc, en dernière analyse, comme la physiologie, qu'un chapitre de la physique et de la chimie. Ces larges assises de la science future de l'esprit survivront sans doute à bien des constructions plus ambitieuses, bâties sur le sable mouvant des systèmes, non sur le roc inébranlable de l'observation et de l'expérience" (*Histoire des doctrines de psychologie physiologique contemporaines. Les Fonctions du cerveau; doctrines de l'école de Strasbourg, doctrines de l'école italienne,* Paris, 1891, p. 391).
"Le travail cérébral est une forme de l'énergie. L'intelligence a des équivalents chimiques, thermiques, mécaniques" (*Les Fonctions du cerveau,* p. 395).

[9] Soury (*Fonctions,* p. 354 and note 1) quotes R. Ardigo: "Le cours des événements psychiques est absolument fatal, ni plus ni moins que celui de tous les événements de la nature" ("La Science expérimentale de la pensée," *Revue scientifique,* April 27, 1889).

[10] "La seule distinction spécieuse qu'on pourrait faire entre les mouvements de l'organisme serait celle de conscients et d'inconscients, distinction d'ailleurs admise et maintenue par Goltz. Mais la conscience n'est qu'un état, un épiphénomène: ce n'est pas plus un être que la volonté" (*Les Fonctions du cerveau,* p. 127).
Soury attacks the belief that there are such "spiritual entities" in the functioning of intelligence as "attention," "will," "consciousness," or

Soury even believed, in agreement with the ideas of Alexandre Herzen, that consciousness was a state of imperfect organic development and that cerebral activity might in time become a subconscious automatism. Without going so far, Barrès was quite prepared to belittle the intelligence or hear it decried,[11] since his belief that the authentic Self resided in a spontaneous and at times unconscious will effectively bypassed intelligence. The yardstick of man's true nature was no longer his intelligence, but rather the instinctive force within him.

It would be a mistake, however, to think that Barrès was systematically contemptuous of intelligence. He was well aware that he was an "intellectual" whose experience of life had been formed by books and ideas. Intelligence, for him, was a tool and not an end in itself. It could not provide truth, but it could devise the method for finding it. Thus he is contemptuous of intelligence when it is divorced from the profound sources of creative energy within the Self; when, as in the Temple of Wisdom

---

"character." These are rather effects than causes: "Mais, comme tous les états de l'esprit, comme toutes les fonctions de l'organisme, l'attention est un effet tout autant qu'une cause; elle accompagne certains processus du cerveau avec lesquels elle apparaît et disparaît; elle est l'aspect interne, psychique, conscient, d'un phénomène biologique dont les conditions physico-chimiques sont pour nous l'explication ultime" (*Les Fonctions du cerveau*, p. 139).

[11] Barrès insists, like Cabanis and Soury, that the intelligence is dependent upon the sensations of the physical organs and he, too, sees intelligence as an "epiphinomenon": "Le concept le plus métaphysique, le plus élevé, la Justice par exemple, n'est fondamentalement, quand on considère ses ingrédients, qu'un composé de simples sensations aux modifications du tégument cutané des muqueuses et des appareils périphériques de l'olfaction, du goût, etc.

Une fonction, c'est un organe en activité... l'intelligence n'existe pas, c'est une résultante, c'est une fonction de résultat. C'est le cerveau en activité" (*Mes Cahiers*, I, 90).

Victor Brombert writes: "Barrès liked to parade his contempt for intelligence as well. Impressed by some remarks made by the physiologist, Jules Soury, he waxed lyrical about the grandeur of "uncultivated life" (he of all people!) and repeated by heart, like a conscientious schoolboy: 'Intelligence! ... what a tiny thing at the very surface of our personality!' Behind this attempt to discredit the intelligence of the 'simian mammal' (a pet expression of Jules Soury), it is easy to detect a reaction against the rationalistic tradition with its faith in science and progress, and its intellectual cosmopolitanism" (*The Intellectual Hero, Studies in the French Novel. 1880-1955*, Philadelphia and New York, J. B. Lippincott, 1961, p. 26).

in *Sous l'œil des barbares,* it is just a sterile activity turning upon itself.[12] He defines the essential characteristic of man — that which separates him from other animals — as the ability to "set his sensations intelligently in order" (SVM p. 268). When Barrès places himself before his own feelings, before a landscape, or before a work of art, it is not to abandon himself to any intellectual surrender. On the contrary, by reflection and analysis, he attempts to uncover the real significance of the phenomenon. But the truth itself is not a logical, rational proposition. It engages the whole man, not just his head; it is rooted in the psycho-physiological totality of the human animal. Thus the truth is embodied, in Barrès' universe, by creatures (women and animals) whose intelligence is least developed, whose grasp on life and awareness of that truth are instinctive and physical.

However much he may seem to downgrade intelligence and to celebrate the Unconscious, he never attempts to give his readers any direct apprehension of the spontaneous life force. The mystery of Bérénice is decomposed and rearranged into a thematic spectrum through the lucid prism of Philippe's mind. His books are a bringing to consciousness of intuitively experienced underlying truths. Intelligence has been dethroned, but intensity of consciousness remains a major value. In his comments on the rank of intelligence in the hierarchy of human values, Barrès adopts a position which is close in some ways to that of Proust and Gide after him. These three writers can only be classed as intellectuals; they are the product of a highly refined culture and their thought and style always bear the marks of a great subtlety of mind, but all

---

[12] A common idea in the second half of the 19th century was that the age was suffering from an excess of cerebrality. Analysis, consciousness, and thought were felt to be diseases of the imagination. Barrès' main quarrel with intelligence was this sterilizing and paralyzing effect upon the soul. He considered that it had developed as a parasite of sensibility during the 19th century. He wrote of the "empiètement incessant de l'intelligence sur la sensibilité" (*Les Taches d'encre*, p. 458). He saw the accentuation of Romantic sickness as a result of the development of lucid analysis: "Nous flétrissons de notre analyse les dernières et les plus exquises sentimentalités" ("Le Sentiment en littérature," *Les Taches d'encre*, p. 451).

However, Barrès always considered himself an *analyst* in this special sense of the word as a man who is continually observing and dissecting his own feelings.

of them in their different ways assert the primacy of sensation and immediacy.

So Philippe and Simon begin their retreat in Saint-Germain by a physical examination in the course of which the doctor finds them "delicate, but healthy" (HL p. 43) and helps them to establish the relation between their character and their physical constitution. Simon is dominated by bilio-nervousness. He needs plenty of fresh air and exercise to stay fit, but the sedentary life of the city produces a grave unbalance by overstimulating his nerves on the one hand and slowing down his epigastric system and his circulation on the other. His energy and enthusiasm are thus subject to sudden flights and he has difficulty in transforming his desires into action (HL pp. 45-46). Philippe finds that he was born with the constitution which Simon had acquired in the city: "Chez moi, d'une activité musculaire toujours nulle, le système cérébral et nerveux a tout accaparé" (p. 46). As a result, his physical organs have developed unequally and in some cases have ceased to function healthily: it was his stomach which went first, he says.

The egotist's program is thus conceived as a remedy for a sickly physique and an unhealthy imagination. In contrast to the uniqueness of his endeavor in which he takes so much pride, his mental and physical constitution is a "well-known phenomenon" (p. 46). He is typical of a whole generation of young Frenchmen whose energies had been channelled into sterile excesses of the imagination through lack of exercise and too much intellectual activity. In fact, they are all the victims of their experiences in the colleges and *lycées* of France. Long hours of reading, confinement, monotony, and indifferent food were certain to turn an already delicate boy into a sickly, bilious creature. The familiar Barresian themes of solitude, impotence, feverishness, sickness, and nervous irritation can be traced in part to the condition of the hypersensitive schoolboy. *Le Culte du moi* is marked throughout by this precocious and one-sided intellectual development which was the lot of so many young Frenchmen. Cerebral stimulation produced a devouring sense of power in the adolescent, a hunger for the possession of the universe which was in such unhealthy contrast to the impossibility of physical or social expression of his energy. Ambition, dreams of literary glory, and the most ephemeral hope of all: escape into the magnificent destiny of superior feeling, the temptation of Madame Bovary, were the sensitive adolescent's reaction to his isolation in the dusty, dreary schools. In Barrès' work, the distance between the lonely schoolboy self and the unlimited demands of intellectual appetite is at the origin of an anguished tension across the poles of negation and assertion.

Sickness has several thematic functions in *Le Culte du moi*. It provides a kind of analogy with other major themes, so that, although presented literally as something from which Philippe actually suffers, its function is really metaphoric. Sickness can be related to the notion of romantic sickness, to spiritual disgust, and to depression. Romantic sickness, which is an affliction of the mind, is literalized by its association with real, physical disorders. The very notion of sickness to characterize the romantic imagination is itself metaphoric to some extent, and this metaphoric element is treated literally by Barrès. This tendency is, of course, related to the theories of psycho-physiology which aim at reducing moral phenomena to their physical origins. It is not irrelevant, in this context, to remember that decadence was taken literally by some in this period. Thinkers believed in a real physical decline among the overcivilized peoples, of which decadent art was only one symptom. Historical thinking had, in its increasing pessimism, taken over the current scientific interest in degeneration.

The idea of cultural sickness was thus taken literally towards the end of the 19th Century, by Barrès and others. There was a preoccupation with hygiene which affected personal, social, and political life. Colonialism, physical action, adventure, the boy-scout movement, nationalist and racial doctrine to name a few, were manifestations of a desire to purify and reinvigorate what was felt as a diseased civilization. The romantic legacy of hypersensitivity is treated as a physical disorder by Barrès, to be remedied by appropriate hygienic measures. Thus in *Sous l'œil des barbares:*

> Silencieux et affaissé, il cachait le plus possible ses sentiments, mais la meilleure réfutation qu'il leur connût consistait en un long bain vers dix heures du soir et une préparation de chloral (p. 250).

The irony which hinges on the deviation of the word *réfutation* from its expected meaning of rational argument to become the equivalent of remedy, lies in the equation of his feelings with mere physical symptoms.

The frequent allusions to hygiene and medecine taking in the first two books of the trilogy not only reinforce the general theme of unhealthiness; they also contribute to this sort of ironic undercutting. As the young man in *Sous l'œil des barbares* walks desolately through the streets of Paris weighing his despair, he indulges in some phantasies of possible hygienic steps he could take if he were to abandon his solitary existence. He would install an excellent cook to make him fine meals in a cool kitchen where he could go and flip through manuals of hygiene while sipping a glass of quinine water (SB pp. 269-70). On another occasion, he follows in his imagination the course of his dinner through his body:

> Nous autres analyseurs, songeait-il, rien de ce qui se passe en nous ne nous échappe. Je vois distinctement de petits morceaux de rosbif qui bataillent, hideux et rouges, dans mon tube digestif (SB p. 248).

The ironic literalization of the phrase "nothing that happens inside us" reduces his moral anguish to a purely physical nightmare. If Barrès reminds the reader of René when he meditates ecstatically upon the ruins of the past, who can imagine René worrying whether he will digest the lobster he had for lunch (HL p. 7)?

At the beginning of *Un Homme libre,* Philippe recounts the evolution of his sensibility in the years before he met Simon. He tells how he entered the world of law, literature, and politics, quite without convictions, but endowed with his natural lucidity and a good knowledge of Stendhal:

> Je puis dire qu'en six mois, je fis un long chemin. J'observais mal l'hygiène, je me dégoûtai, je partis; puis je revins, ayant bu du quinquina et adorant Renan. Je dus encore m'absenter; les larmoiements idéalistes cédèrent aux petits faits de Sainte-Beuve. En 86, je pris du bromure; je ne pensais plus qu'à moi-même. Dyspepsique, un peu hypocondriaque, j'appris avec plaisir que Simon souffrait de coliques néphrétiques (pp. 5-6).

The alternation of references to Stendhal, Renan, and Sainte-Beuve with details about his health problems has the effect of deflating the whole course of his own intellectual development. At the same time, this self-disparagement is accompanied by a note of cockiness or flippancy which is so characteristic of *Un Homme libre*.

It is in Baudelaire's *Journaux intimes* once again that the theme of hygiene may have its origin: the second part of this work is called "Hygiène." Feeling himself threatened by insanity, Baudelaire lists the steps he takes in a program of moral and physical hygiene. Like Barrès' hero, he resorts to medicaments and remedial baths: "Poisson, bains froids, douches, lichen, pastilles occasionnellement; d'ailleurs suppression de tout excitant." [13] A striking similarity between "Hygiène" and *Un Homme libre* is the association of bodily hygiene and religious discipline, especially, prayer, in a wider hygiene of the soul. Of the three provisions in Baudelaire's program, only work is absent from Barrès' novel. Like Philippe, Baudelaire establishes a series of rules to govern the course of his life:

> Je me jure à moi-même de prendre désormais les règles suivantes pour règles éternelles de ma vie: Faire tous les matins ma prière à Dieu, réservoir de toute force et de toute justice, à mon père, à Mariette et à Poe, comme intercesseurs. [14]

Even the notion of method, which is so important in *Un Homme libre*, occurs in the *Journaux intimes:* two of the sub-sections in "Hygiène" are entitled "Hygiène, Conduite, Méthode." [15]

The complaints from which Philippe suffers are minor, symptomatic of a poor general condition. They affect the stomach and the nervous system for the most part: poor digestion, biliousness, colic, anemia, nevralgia, insomnia, migraine. These afflictions are appropriate because in most people's experience (particularly in France where nervousness and digestive problems are almost traits of national character) they do reveal a certain interdependence

---

[13] *Œuvres complètes*, p. 1269.
[14] Ibid., pp. 1269-70.
[15] Ibid., p. 1268 and p. 1269.

of the moral and physical states. Barrès always presents himself to his reader as a sickly man, with an extremely capricious gastric system which serves as a physical indicator of his emotional state. Extreme nervousness lies on the borderline between a real, physical deficiency of the nervous system and the temperamental constitution of the moral character. It partakes of both and serves as a link between the physical and the moral elements.

The feeling of depression is usually accompanied by these physical afflictions. As is true in the works of Hysmans,[16] the obsession with food, digestion, and remedies parallels the sense of horror which life inspires in the sensitive man. In *Sous l'œil des barbares,* the young man suffers an attack of nevralgia as his emotional anguish reaches a peak. He feels himself literally poisoned by the "vulgar universe," menaced by biliousness and "coliques hépatiques" (pp. 260-261); he is troubled by rhumatism (p. 263) and threatened by anemia (p. 266). On the train for Saint-Germain, Philippe remarks: "Malgré que l'odeur de la houille et les visages des voyageurs toujours me bouleversent l'estomac, l'avenir me paraissait désirable" (HL p. 15). The rhetorical linking of two causes of quite a different order reduces moral revulsion to the level of physical nausea.

These details concerning the body have no fictional relevance; they do not contribute to the unfolding of any story or to the exploration of character. They are given such prominence because they function metaphorically within the total thematic complex. Of course, actual metaphors or comparisons often emerge from this relationship:

> Ces querelles émoussées, ces compliments, ces réclamations m'étaient une chose de dégoût, comme l'idée fixe dans l'anémie cérébrale, ou, dans l'indigestion, le fumet des viandes qui la causèrent (JB pp. 186-187).

But whether the symptoms are literally experienced by the egotist or are simply evoked to say what his feelings were like, the effect

---

[16] Especially in *A vau-l'eau* where M. Folantin's monotonous and insipid existence is represented as an endlessly frustrated search for a restaurant in which his flagging appetite may be revived. In this book, lack of appetite is the sign of a spiritual impotence which empties life of all appeal.

is the same. In this kind of non-realist novel, story motifs function on the axis of metaphorical significance and not on the plane of fictional illusions.

It is often the case in Barrès' writing that his images are subordinated to the thematic organization in this way, growing out of a previously established analogy or identification. The religious images emerge in *Un Homme libre* out of the essential thematic association of the cult of the Self with the adoration of a God. Similarly, the numerous images of mechanism develop from the notion of mechanical and artificial stimulation of feeling. Since the processes of the mind are interpreted as a biological mechanism, the relation between tenor and vehicle is more than just one of suggestiveness: there is a material similarity. This tendency to literalization has the effect of blurring the distinction between the literal and the figurative and, at the same time, of reducing moral phenomena to their physical equivalents.

Elsewhere we find the young egotist in such a state of feverish hypersensitivity that he experiences tingling sensations all over his body — "an intolerable acuity" (HL p. 136). In the course of his experiment with the "Object" in Chapter Eleven, Philippe's nervous anxiety attains a paroxysm of physical tension in which he feels like kicking the furniture or smashing plates and which gives an idea of what it is to be an epileptic (pp. 219-20). [17] This feverishness is one of Barrès' most characteristic conditions, and its value is ambivalent in *Le Culte du moi*. Sickness and fever may be the symptoms of unhappiness, depression, and emotional instability, but they are also the origin of his exaltations. Periods of intense feeling are associated with sickness and good health with reduced awareness and a flat commonplace vision of the world. He is only truly himself in these hours of unhealthy ex-

---

[17] Barrès was well aware of the literature of "énervement" and neurosis which characterized the more frenetic works of the period. He describes Sainte-Beuve's *Volupté* as the "most enervating of masterpieces," (*Les Taches d'encre,* p. 393). We should note that this "enervating" quality is clearly a virtue. In this same essay ("La Folie de Charles Baudelaire"), he writes: "C'est bien la tradition des sataniques, continuée aujourd'hui par des esprits analogues, par M. Maurice Rollinat, qui nous apparaît foudroyé, yeux fulgurants, cheveux hirsutes, en tête de son volume les *Névroses;* par les *Poèmes saturniens* et les *Poètes maudits,* de M. Paul Verlaine; par le *Guignon,* de M. Stéphane Mallarmé" (p. 391).

citement. Barrès is typical of his generation in preferring the superior realm of the anxious spirit, however diseased his analysis may show it to be, to the mediocrity of bourgeois normality.

At the beginning of *Un Homme libre,* Philippe declares: "Le paradis c'est d'être clairvoyant et fiévreux" (p. 22). A little earlier, he had explained to Simon:

> Notre vertu la moins contestable, c'est d'être clairvoyants, et nous sommes en même temps ardents avec délire. Chez nous, l'apaisement n'est que débilité; il a toute la tristesse du malade qui tourne la tête contre le mur (p. 13).

The desired state of ardor is thus equated with fever, but the delirium which accompanies it is something that increases the lucidity of the mind. It is by no means a blurring of consciousness; there is no invasion of hallucinatory dreams. On the contrary, feverishness is an excitement of the brain which emotionally charges the lucid and coldly analytic vision. It usually has a positive value: "Cette pensée lui fut une sensation si complète de sa douleur, qu'il atteignit à cette sorte de joie du fiévreux enfin seul, grelottant sous ses couvertes" (p. 108). The image of acute unhappiness as a physical sensation akin to a high fever reinforces the idea, so essential to Barrès' work, that thought and sensation are equivalent. By abandoning himself, almost voluptuously, to his solitary misery, he experiences a joy in the self-indulgent intensification of his feelings. Feverishness and exaltation are almost identical in that they overcome the sterility which threatens the abstract intelligence. The image of the sick man turning his face to the wall translates the emptiness of resignation. Sickness should intensify the responses of the mind and of the body. It is defeat when it leads to a dulling of the senses. Among the sins which the egotists proscribe in their cult of the Self is "lack of fever," associated with everything that is gray and tepid. Fever, of course, is often used simply to mean "passion" or "violent enthusiasm," the equivalent of "ardor" in its Gidian sense, but its thematic association with literal sickness confers a double resonance upon the term. Sickness appears, then, in *Le Culte du moi* as a value, as something to be cultivated for the heightened sensibility which accompanies it. The hypersensitivity of his nerves is a guarantee of emotional intensity, by carrying to the extreme all his sensations, even the most unpleasant, so that they take on the stature of noble passions. Feverishness leads him back to emotional fullness by exacerbating his despair.

As Barrès writes in the Preface to *Un Homme libre:* "Souvent leurs maladies préparent leur santé" (p. xi), similarly Philippe defines his project as "la culture de [ses] inquiétudes" (HL p. 19). He underlines the relation between his sickness and the method which will lead to the creation of his universe. His feeling of disgust, that delicate reaction which makes him recoil from the vulgarity of the world around him, has a function within the framework of his method. It acts as a preventive remedy (he speaks of his "dégoût préventif" [HL p. 19]) against the loss of the Self among the temptations that surround it. Furthermore the egotist intends to utilize the afflictions of his mind and body in the creation of his embellished universe. On the one hand they are a guarantee of authenticity because they are truly his own and not borrowed attitudes, and on the other the possibility of a cure can be hoped for in the deliberate cultivation of these weaknesses. The descent into the Self is a therapeutic probe which does not seek to remove the disease so much as to bring it into the light of consciousness so that the symptoms can be assimilated into a new total health.

The entire Cult of the Self can be seen, then, as a form of therapy, as a "hygiene of the soul" (HL p. 39) similar to that perfected by the religious orders. Thus when the young man exclaims at the end of *Sous l'œil des barbares:* "Maître qui guérirait de la sécheresse" (p. 271), the verb *guérir* is to be taken almost literally in its physical sense. Bérénice's obscure solidarity with her race and the world around her is a "strong medication" (JB p. 100) for Philippe. Her function is to incarnate many of the diseased aspects of his sensibility (melancholy, love of solitude, nostalgic dreaming), but in such a way that they are transformed into creative values.

The creation of a personal "Lorraine" is thus ultimately a "hygienic" construction in which the egotist finds health by merging himself with an organic entity of which he is a living part, but which is greater than the Self. If individualism is felt as unhealthy, it is by a conscious exaggeration of it that a cure may be effected. It serves as the basis for self-discovery. By carrying individualism to the extreme, Barrès finds that it has no meaning outside the racial continuity which made it possible. True individualism can only be conscious acceptance of group identity. In this way, health, spiritual energy, and an authentic basis for action are restored. When he associated the absolute, religious, value attributed to the adoration of the Self with the notion of hygiene, he was indicating the temporary nature of his cult of individualism as a therapeutic interlude.

The same literalization can be observed in Barrès' treatment of the words *goûter* and *appétit*. His starting point is the common usage of the word appetite to mean spiritual hunger or desire. Since desire is the most authentic expression of our innermost being, appetite, suggesting the basic instinctual urge, is an appropriate term for it within Barrès' system. The same is true of the verb *goûter*, a word which occurs with great frequency in his writing as an important element in the vocabulary of egotism. The enjoyment of emotion is reduced to the level of sensation, by association with the literal meaning of the word. As Philippe begins to meditate upon the Lorraine of his ancestors, he says: "Je me découvrais une sensibilité nouvelle et profonde qui me parut savoureuse" (HL p. 93). This revival of the metaphorical significance of *goûter* is carried even further in the following text where Barrès explains why André was fasciné by Marina: "Elle était un ragoût extrêmement savoureux et bien fait pour saisir l'imagination d'un homme exigeant et hautain dans ses désirs" (EL p. 66). André finds her quite literally "to his taste."

Barrès uses this technique of literal reduction to satirize his teachers in *Sous l'œil des barbares*. The "Bonhomme Système," holding forth on how to live among the ruins of vanished idéals, confides his own formula to the young man:

> Satisfaisons nos appétits, de quelque nom que les glorifie ou les invective le vulgaire. Je vous le dirai en confidence, mon ami, je n'aime plus guère à cette heure que les viandes grillées vivement cuites et les déclamations un peu courtes (pp. 22-23).

The "Bonhomme Système" continues in this vein, referring to "ces fins régals d'analyste" (p. 76) and describing the pleasures of expansion as "cette tisane du noctambule" (p. 76). He talks of the "appetite of friendship" (p. 76) and depicts the meeting of two friends as two dogs sniffing each other (p. 77). Man's sensibility is likened to frogs croaking in the subconscious (p. 77) and love is no more than a sport to be practised as a remedy for overeating (p. 78).

Another illustration of how Barrès attains his effects by playing on the literal and figurative meanings of *appétit* and *goûter* is a passage from Chapter Four of *L'Ennemi des lois*. In their search for the conditions of a complete mental reform by which the theories of social transformation could be assimilated to the modern sensibility, André and Claire go to Germany. André finds that German socialism is essentially the political expression of the basic needs of the masses. Socialism, he reflects, has reduced the more widely ambitious doctrines of the French *Idéologues* to a purely material, economic doctrine: "le socialisme a paru réduire le parti des idéologues au parti du ventre" (p. 149). Since his own appetite is rather frugal, he is unable to sympathize immediately with this vision of future happiness as a "kermesse" or to reduce his idealistic ardor to "a campaign for the stomach" (p. 150). Food has thus been taken quite literally as the basic objective in the revolutionary program of the socialist masses. However, by equating food with the objectives of social reform, Barrès is really creating a metonymic image: the part for the whole— food representing physical well-being in general.

He complicates this notion, which could apply to the social aspirations of any country, by introducing the commonplace prejudice against Germans as stolid, unimaginative dumpling eaters. Shortly afterwards, André experiences this Germanic awareness of the stomach after a heavy, rather greasy meal in a Munich restaurant (pp. 151-152). He admires the German people for their "good taste" in providing sharp, sour things to eat after the roast. André is now more willing to admit that the stomach can be the "sensitive point" which determines a people's attitudes to life. From these physical observations, he goes on to generalize about the German ideal as compared to the French:

> Chez nous, Français, la dominante, c'est la vanité; de là notre rêve: égalité, notre cri: justice. Ici, c'est l'appétit;

de là leur rêve: bien-être, leur cri: améliorations matérielles (p. 152).

In his continued efforts to penetrate the Germanic spirit, André turns to their works of art, convinced that there is a relation between the ideals of a people and the kind of art they produce (p. 153). He meditates upon a painting by Cranach, in which the female figures, although they evoke the atmosphere of Germany, also remind him of Marina. He observes the same material sensuality that fascinated him in the title Russian princess. This is the point of empathy which enables him to better appreciate the culture of Germany.

> Ainsi l'image de Marina, évoquée dans l'atmosphère allemande, l'illuminait pour André. Alors qu'il s'épaississait avec ces socialistes qui préparent le bonheur futur comme un festin de noce, le souvenir de Marina fut une goutte d'ammoniaque versée dans son verre à la suite d'un repas trop lourd, et qui restitue à l'esprit sa lucidité (p. 155).

Thus the observation he made in the Munich restaurant is picked up as a metaphor. The literal reflections on appetite and taste are now applied figuratively to his ability to appreciate (*goûter*) the Germanic spirit. Marina, by providing the acid contrast after the heaviness of his ruminations on German socialism, corrects André's limited conception of that doctrine as merely a basely material appetite which will deaden the palate.[18]

A basic idea in *L'Ennemi des lois* is that material appetite has an underlying spiritual value. In several anecdotes, Barrès describes the gluttony of the little girls in the convent school where Marina has been a boarder. On one occasion during the Christmas celebrations, when the big girls, the teachers, and the supervisors are at midnight Mass, the very little ones, who are supposed to be in bed, get up and, pooling their provisions of holiday delicacies, proceed to have a feast. Their selfish greed may be in shocking contrast to the solemnity of the Mass, but Barrès concludes that their ecstasy, although purely physical, is just as much to be valued as any mystical one (pp. 155-57). In a typical Bar-

---

[18] Inversely André reflects: "Lui-même, à cet instant, pour percevoir la saveur florentine, n'eût-il pas dû se dégraisser le palais!" (El, p. 162).

resian reduction, mystical exaltation is equated with intense physical pleasure. It is the intensity of the feeling which constitutes its value, and not its absolute merits as compared with other more or less "noble" emotions. The little girls' self-indulgent joy is exemplary because it is sincere and unreflecting. André sees an analogy between the charming sensuality of Marina and her schoolfriends and the mentality of the German people. In both the gluttony of the little girls and the socialist demands of the masses, he finds the same "naive sensibility, composed of material appetites and free instincts" (p. 155), and the same qualities of spontaneous self-assertion. A further analogy, this time with the dog Velu, reinforces the message:

> Ce qui justifie de leurs vulgaires revendications ces pesants Bavarois, c'est qu'ils ont l'élan naïf, l'angoisse du Velu en face d'une assiette qui fume et qu'on lui interdit (p. 157).

This statement, although metaphoric in form, is taken as a factual analogy, in view of the context, in which Barrès has reduced socialist ideal literally to the hunger instinct.

Thus he establishes an interplay between the literal and figurative meanings of food and eating, linking the ideological debate to the characters and underlining their exemplary role as sources of analogies and illustrations for abstractions. We have an example of the tapestry-like composition, the intricate give and take between the literal fictional level and the intellectual content, the themes repeated and developed in complex formal patterns the result of which is that stylized reduction of reality where abstract notions are transformed into immediate moral values that can be apprehended by the senses. It is possible to see in the passage that has just been analyzed the function, ideological and stylistic, of Barrès' literalizations and reductions of moral phenomena. By reducing moral entities to their physical equivalents, whether it be in his treatment of the diseased romantic sensibility and the accompanying sense of moral revulsion or in his treatment of the nature of desire, he is searching for the guarantee of authenticity which can only found in the most basic instinctual responses of the senses to the world. The physical demands of the body are a legitimate defense of the Self. Since the egotist has rejected all intellectual and moral guidelines, he must reduce his vision of the world to its basic essentials. He must rediscover the bedrock of authentic self-assertion and build from there. There is certainly in Barrès' reductions and in his willingness to utilize the most banal and even puerile experiences a deliberate attempt to break away from the impotence and oversophistication of an intellectually exhausted era.

On the stylistic level — and of course style and ideology are intimately interrelated — these reductions conform to the principle which Philippe announced in *Un Homme libre:* "Réduisons l'abstrait en images sensibles" (p. 58). The abstract content of socialist ideology is reduced to the most concrete terms by the literalization of the notion of appetite in the particularized anecdotes from Marina's past. The gap between the two may seem enormous, but Barrès is deliberately cultivating it. The trivial sentimentality of the anecdotes in connection with political ideology is intended to surprise, even to annoy, the reader, but it brings home his main point, which is that intellectual commitment is insufficient. To act effectively for social reform, the individual must sympathize with his whole being with the ends to be attained. For these general goals to become real to the individual, he must reduce them to particular experiences which are relevant and authentic for him.

The reader cannot help being struck, then, by the excessive, even simplistic quality of some of these passages. I believe this to be quite deliberate on Barrès' part, in accordance with an attitude which he adopts throughout the early works. Satire, self-irony, provocation of the reader, and a genuine desire to discover a new form of sincerity are essential ingredients in his very peculiar and often very subtle non-conformism. The tendency to remind the reader of the body and bring things down to a physical level has an important function in the early works. First of all, these reductions serve as we have seen, to undercut the emotional flights of his hypersensitive temperament and they contribute thereby to the essential *self-possession* and *self-control* which are the foundations of the Barresian attitude. The irony is directed towards himself in a systematic self-disparagement which is the measure of the egotist's detachment from the contingent aspects of his being. However, the full force of a certain insistence in his works upon the body as a source of humiliation (and even as an object of humiliation) can only be felt in the context of the theme of self-pity and its various allegorical projections. This will be the subject of my next chapter.

Secondly, the irony of these reductions is directed outwards as a satirical deflation of the attitudes and ways of thinking which encumber his moral universe. It plays a major part in the demolitional enterprise by which Barrès attempts to level the terrain in preparation for a new start and a new construction. It is linked to the principal theme of *Le Culte du moi,* which is that, in the absence of any certainty, one must start from oneself, that one must refer everything to the most elementary needs of the Self, and that one must reduce everything to its most basic expression. In this sense, his egotism itself is a form of radical reduction. In its early manifestations, its real thrust is ironic and critical, rather than an expression of any profound "self-centeredness." That is to say, it is an instrument rather than an end in itself. The third function of these reductions, beyond any satirical intent, is related to the techniques of Barrès' "ideological" demonstrations. They are a means of concretizing or rendering assimilable certain moral truths and, in this, they are in turn closely related with the techniques of personification and allegory.

CAPTER IV

THE ALLEGORIES OF THE SELF

The egotist, assured that the "real" world is only phenomenal appearance proceeds to create an artificial universe in which his subjectivity can develop most completely. He substitutes a reduced reality which reflects his own nature and includes only such elements of the outside world as can adapt themselves to the categories of his soul. This universe is allegorical first of all in the sense that it is the projection of the Self. Barrès affirms this himself in the *Examen* when he states that Bérénice is the feminine part of himself: "A-t-on remarqué que la femme est la même à travers ces trois volumes, accommodée simplement au milieu?" (*Examen*, p. 31). The young girl in *Sous l'œil des barbares*, he says, is already Bérénice and so is the "Object" in *Un Homme libre*. In fact, the name "Object" is the one which is most suited to her: "Elle est, en effet, objectivée, la part sentimentale qu'il y a dans un jeune homme de ce temps" (p. 32). She is the projection of his sensibility, adapted in each of her manifestations to the "environment," by which he means the thematic context. Thus, in the first novel of the trilogy, she represents the attraction of sensual contact with the world, the Ideal, and the life of the Dandy. In *Le Jardin de Bérénice*, she is thematically related to his political inquiry into the possibility of understanding and acting upon the soul of the people. Her function as Marina is similarly linked to a social issue in *L'Ennemi des lois*.

On a second level, then, the allegories are ideological — representations of abstract ideas. In the figures of Bérénice and the other female creatures who embody his instinctive sensuality, his romantic tendencies, and even his most trivial sentimentality, he indulges his intimate phantasies; but at the same time they relay back to the egotist an objective moral lesson. Knowledge about the world is acquired through observation of the Self. Through the allegorical figure of Bérénice, the young egotist learns the qualities which are the political strength of the people: instinctive sensuality, spontaneity, unconscious identification with the world, awareness of the past, a sense of continuity in tradition, and a melancholy regret which is projected into the future as a nameless desire. She is *Petite Secousse,* the irrepressible urge of the lifeforce striving unconsciously but infallibly to create the future. She accepts the world as it is, but she represents the force through which all authentic change appears in the world. The people, with their innate sense of race and continuity, are a source of spiritual health, a therapeutic bath for the intellectual debilitated by individualism.

Thus the universe, situated half way between the Self and the outside world, is more than just a sterile esthetic reflection of the individual. Certainly his universe is a form of self-adornment, but the purpose of its beauty is to illuminate the outside world so that the antagonism between the Self and exterior reality is eliminated. He learns that the Self and the world are similar, obeying the same laws and striving towards the same self-realization. He reveals the source of creative energy within himself and within the world: the instinctive urge for growth and fulfillment which desires the future while remaining faithful to the past. Thus, in the terms of his system, there is no contradiction between his doctrine of racial continuity and the absolute individualism of his inner cult.

Here, I think, the relation between Barrès' cult of emotion and moral truth is apparent. On the one hand, emotion is held to be the proper end of the universe, to such an extent that one can see Barrès as a dilettante of emotion. Yet everything in *Le Culte du moi* converges on the moral truth which it contains. In the absence of any other certitude, the authenticity of truly personal feeling is the source of all truth. For him, to know is to be moved. Thus, dilettantism becomes in effect the egotist's moral guide, since the cultivation of emotion leads him to an intuition of the moral laws of life. Emotion is converted into fruitful moral attitudes which can eventually be diverted towards life and action in the world.

We have often seen that Barrès deliberately descends into triviality in his treatment of the body and its ailments, and in his use of rather puerile anecdotes centered around Marina. Philippe often complains, in *Un Homme libre,* of his feeling of mediocrity; he despises his own inadequacy and he is also quite aware of the puerility of his enterprise which he refers to contemptuously as "tout ce cabotinage supérieur" (p. 76). In the elaboration of the fundamental axiom of this novel: "Il faut sentir le plus possible en analysant le plus possible," he explains that the weakest sensation can provide great joy when we analyse it with someone who sympathizes with us. And even humiliating emotions can become voluptuous when they are transformed into thought. The idea that insignificant emotions are as worthy of cultivation as the most sublime, and may indeed be the only ones they are capable of enjoying, is confirmed by the results of their psycho-physiological examination.

> De cet état [their melancholy disposition], disent les médecins, sortent des passions tristes, minutieuses, personnelles, des idées petites, étroites et portant sur les objets des plus légères sensations. Et la vie s'écoule, pour ces sujets, dans une succession de petites joies et de petits chagrins qui donnent à toute leur manière d'être un caractère de puérilité (p. 47).

This, then, is the raw material with which they have to work. It is not very inspiring in itself, but the important thing, as Barrès constantly reminds himself, is to stimulate the emotional mechanism so that the reflective faculties can begin to function. The slightest emotion, when it is taken up and "replayed" in the lucidity of consciousness, can be deepened into a meaningful experience. The portraits of his female figures are composed in large part of these "little joys and little sorrows" which create an atmosphere of rather puerile sentimentality around them.

In application of this principle, Philippe evolves a complete theory of anecdotes. At the very beginning of *Un Homme libre,* he remarks on his practice of jotting down his sensations on a little notebook so that they can be recaptured "when time has blunted them" (p. 20). To do this, he attaches his emotions to the events, however banal, which give rise to them, and then, by reviving the concrete reality of these circumstances (Loyola's method at work), he is able to recover "at will" the sensations that accompany them:

> Et pour ce, rattachons-la, fût-elle de l'ordre métaphysique le plus haut, à quelque objet matériel que nous puissions toucher jusque dans nos pires dénuements (HL. p. 58).

One such memory, which he cites as an example, is of a troop of soldiers marching in the street. The exhilarating sound of the trumpets inspires him in his own proud desire to control his emotional mechanism, just as the officer controls the men in his command (pp. 20-21). The little scene has a metaphoric relevance to his moral situation, and comes, in memory, to embody a lesson. This can perhaps be considered again as a tendency to allegorize, since specific events in the real world serve as illustrations for moral considerations.

The world is reduced to a system of signs, of high emotional value, to be deciphered according to their significance for the personal reality of the Self. Elaborating on the role of anecdotes in his universe, Philippe explains:

> Une centaine de petites anecdotes grossières inscrites sur mon carnet me donnent sûrement les rêves les plus exquis que l'humanité puisse concevoir. Elles sont les clochers qui guident le fidèle jusqu'à la chapelle où il s'agenouille (HL p. 62).

Thus he proposes to catalogue and condense the world of emotions into a series of "suggestive rebus" to adorn the walls of his vast inner palace (HL p. 58). Again we find in passages like these the combination of lyrical enthusiasm, calculated arrogance, and brash irony which is so characteristic of *Un Homme libre*.

André, in *L'Ennemi des lois,* proposes that they create a similar book of anecdotes: "un livret, chaques mois, pour faire pleurer" (p. 210). This, he claims, would be far more effective than a treatise on a new morality. They would publish "the most moving anecdotes," taken from the events of everyday life, to demonstrate the cruelty of the world. Each reader would find the anecdote "which melts the aridity of his heart," so that he could apply it to the circumstances of his own life and cry: "Pauvre moi-même" (p. 211). The abstract question of social justice would thus be reduced to an intensely personal awareness.

> Tel que je le conçois, ce petit livre aux nombreux paragraphes alignés, ce sera un vaste hôpital où chacun reconnaîtra sa maladie, où chacun occupera un lit. Nous serons voisins dans la douleur (p. 211).

André's reflections on his little book of anecdotes sound the main theme of the novel: that pity for the suffering of others is only possible when it is translated into concrete terms of self-pity. Since the egotist can know nothing outside of himself, he must establish his contact with the world through authentic points of sympathy. The notion of moral suffering is literalized by the image of the hospital; André's purpose is to create a real community of sufferers — a novel form of socialism!

Going a step further than Philippe, André explicitly assigns a practical moral function to the emotion created by the anecdotes. The emotion, essentially esthetic in as much as it is valued for its beauty, is the key which unlocks the door to fecund moral action in the world: "Voilà l'essentiel: pousser toutes les douleurs en beauté" (pp. 211-12), André concludes. In Barrès' "universe," emotion, beauty, and moral truth are thus indissolubly interrelated. The purpose of this sentimentalizing in *L'Ennemi des lois* is to show how instinct can be a value in social relations. The spontaneous movement of the heart can be the basis of a more abstract solidarity with the suffering and destitute in general. The movement from an emotional or esthetic reaction to a moral value parallels the movement from the closed world of the Self towards the society of other men.

In addition to the mixture of sincerity, arrogant assertion, and self-deflating irony which contribute to the tonal complexity of the early works, there is clearly another note present in all this. There are overtones of a delicious self-pity which cultivates this very mediocrity. Barrès cherishes the touching spectacle of his own humiliated existence. At the origin of this very Barresian form of sentimentality, is his memory of himself as a child. It will be remembered that the "Oraison" at the end of *Sous l'œil des barbares* begins with a passionate affirmation of his fidelity to the child he once was and a poignant reminiscence of the humiliations he suffered in those years (p. 275). This text, together with others which testify to the strength of his attachment to his childhood self and to his sense of an original psychic wound, is essential in understanding the dynamics of the allegorical structure of his works. His narcissism generates a whole mythology of figures representing the wounded and humiliated Self. The allegorical women in his works are always victims of misfortune and humiliation. They are the creatures on whom he projects his own self-pity. The same mechanism is at work in the imaginative construction of his native Lorraine, which is a direct descendant of these earlier humiliated heroines. The historical failure of Lorraine to fully develop its own culture, the decadence of its traditions, the German annexation of part of its territory, and the melancholy of its landscapes arouse the same feelings of pity as the sufferings of Bérénice and Marina. Moreover, by projecting his sensibility in the form of young women, he adds a sensual dimension to the basic emotion of pity. The whole complex of pity, self-pity, and sadism which I shall discuss shortly derives its emotional tension from this initial figure of the wounded Self. Indeed, sexual emotion, at least as expressed in his books, is only possible when linked to this particular form of Self-love.

In the allegorical works, sexual desire is regularly confused with the quite different order of emotions inspired by children. The result is that there is a subtly ambiguous merging of sentimentality and sensuality in these stories. In the portraits that Barrès draws of his heroines, he devotes a great amount of space to details of their childhood, particularly in the case of Bérénice and Marina, his two most developed allegories. Similarly Delrio's great pleasure in *Un Amateur d'âmes,* the first story of *Du sang,* was to question Simone on her impressions when she was a child. The "Object" in *Un Homme libre* is described throughout as a little girl, and indeed she is little more than a sensual and capricious child — "un instinct dansant" (p. 215). Bérénice is a grown woman when the action of *Le Jardin de Bérénice* takes place, but it is always as a child that he sees to her. Philippe first met her when she was still a little girl, a poor little orphan, obliged to dance in a night club to keep herself alive. Chapters III and IV give an account of her upbringing in the allegorical atmosphere of the *Musée du roi René*. Philippe lingers sentimentally on her childhood and the wretched conditions of her existence as a child-whore. He is inspired to evoke memories from his own childhood to describe her effect upon him:

> Cette petite libertine, entrevue à une époque fort maussade de ma vie, m'a laissé une image tendre et élégante, que j'ai serrée de côté, comme jadis ces œufs de Pâques dont les couleurs m'émouvaient si fortement que je ne voulais pas les manger (p. 19).

The image is in fact a little anecdote. The same kind of anecdotal image occurs in *Un Homme libre* during the episode with the "Object". As Philippe reflects on the dangers inherent in his experiments, he remarks:

> C'est le jeu un peu fébrile du pauvre enfant qui, par un jour de pluie, assis dans un coin de la chambre, examine son jouet au risque de le casser — non loin des grandes personnes qui sont, en toutes circonstances, un châtiment imminent (p. 207).

The child lives under the constant menace of the oppressive adult world, with the result that his happiness is fragile and somehow furtive, and for this reason all the more to be treasured. Barrès colors almost all his descriptions of childhood with a nuance of pathos.

Like Bérénice, Marina is a child-woman. For André, she is always the little girl whose humiliations and childish rebellion are described in the "Education de la petite princesse" of Chapter II and in "Le Paradis de la petite princesse" of the following chapter. She is a poor, defenseless creature to be protected, consoled, and cherished for the sentimentality she arouses in him. The same affective use of "petit" characterizes André's feeling for her: "une étrange petite figure d'obstination et d'orgueil" (p. 25), "cette petite femme" (p. 36), "cette petite main de femme" (p. 31). Her function seems to be primarily to provide a source of childhood anecdotes.[1]

There is a tight triangular relationship of analogy between women, children, and animals in Barrès' works. They are assigned the role of incarnating the "natural" creative spontaneity of life.[2]

---

[1] Bernanos, aptly but cruelly, likens Barrès to his own creations: "Paix au Barrès de *Leurs Figures*! Celui que nous aimons est entré dans la mort avec un regard d'enfant fier, et son pauvre sourire crispé de fille pauvre et noble qui ne trouvera jamais de mari" (Preface to *Les Grands Cimetières sous la lune*, Plon, 1938, pp. i-ii).

[2] The notion that there was one unitary force at work in all the phenomena of the material world was, of course, fundamental to much of 19th century scientific and idealist thought. Herbert Spencer just calls it "Force." Cabanis postulates the existence of a unique principle underlying all movement. Like Barrès, he refers to it as "instinct" or "spontaneity" — terms which he applies not just to living beings, but to the organizational properties of all matter. The development of instinct is ascensional, rising through elementary forms of material organization until it reaches the complexities of living beings and eventually intelligence: "Enfin, cet instinct, en se développant de plus en plus, dans ces derniers corps, et parcourant tous les différents degrés d'organisation, ne peut-il pas s'élever jusqu'aux merveilles les plus admirées de l'intelligence et du sentiment" (*Rapports du physique et du moral*, X, p. 531). This idea of an ascending instinctual force is exposed in *Le Jardin de Bérénice* and *L'Ennemi des lois*, where the animals around Bérénice and Marina are portrayed as aspiring unconsciously to a higher state: "Ces canards... et cet âne... et... Bérénice, qu'ils entourent, expriment une angoisse, une tristesse sans borne vers un état de bonheur dont ils se composent une imagination bien confuse, qu'ils placent parfois dans le passé, faisant de leur désir un regret, mais qui est en réalité le degré supérieur au leur dans l'échelle des êtres... En chacun est un être supérieur qui veut se réaliser" (JB, pp. 129-130). Similarly, the lesson of the dog in *L'Ennemi des lois* is that instinctual sensuality and the self-interest that it serves can be surpassed in a higher level of social organization. Individual self-interest is no longer opposed to every other self-interest but functions in the harmony of a mutual consideration based on sympathy for others.

Indeed, Barrès' "socialisme fédéraliste" (of which *L'Ennemi des lois* is an allegorical transposition) is a political counterpart of Cabanis' ascending scale of elective affinities: "Ah! que ne suis-je un grand orateur pour jeter la lumière sur cette ascension de liberté qui, s'élevant de bas en haut, de l'individu libre à la commune libre, permet à la commune de se mouvoir dans la région, épanouit la région dans l'union nationale et fédère la nation elle-même par un lien plus lâche avec les autres États de l'Europe". ("Assainissement et fédéralisme," Librairie de la *Revue socialiste*, 1895, p. 15. Quoted by Victor Giraud, *Les Maîtres de l'heure. Maurice Barrès*, Hachette, 1922, p. 50).

Mme King shows that the influence of Hartmann can be discerned in this notion of ascending instinct: "Comme Hartmann fait sortir l'espèce supérieure de celle qui lui est immédiatement inférieure, en raison

At the end of *L'Ennemi des lois,* he writes: "Toute bête, c'est près de nous, dans une outre agréable à voir, un peu de vie pure de mélange pédant" (p. 248). The lesson of Marina and the dogs is identical: sensuality is a better guide to social justice than the abstract theories of the lawmakers.[3] Egoism can be the motor of social cohesion when the individual learns, through the emotion of pity, that his own needs and desires are a microcosm of the creative instinct of the world, and that he can act in harmony with the greater force of which he is a part. Politically, Barrès is proposing a form of anarchical socialism based on the elective affinities of freely developed, unconstrained individuals. To the objection that, if there were no laws to prevent everyone acting only in his own interest as dogs do, society would be impossible (pp. 238-39), André replies that laws were once necessary as moral crutches but they can be discarded now that men have assimilated the moral code into a social reflex. In the utopian society that they create at the end of the novel, the instruction of children is entrusted to "celui qui ne parle pas," the animal, who will, by his example, show them how to develop their instincts.

Just as the female figures are seen throughout as children, so, too, they are continually reduced to the level of animals — and for much the same reasons. Already in *Sous l'œil des barbares,* the girl was described as an animal: "véritable petit animal d'amour, ingénue et nerveuse" (p. 119), "figure mystérieuse de petit animal nubile" (p. 174). Philippe admits that he cherishes Bérénice above all for her animal simplicity. Her graceful movements (pp. 166-167) and the expression of her eyes (p. 162) are those of a poor young animal. In her death agony, she is compared to an animal curling up to die in a corner of its master's house. Marina, too, is reduced to the level of an instintive animal:

---

des germes de modifications et de perfections qu'elle comporte, Barrès montre comment les animaux les plus bas dans la hiérarchie aspirent vers un état meilleur, tout comme Bérénice en regrettant la mort de son ami, enfante quelque chose qui sera mieux qu'elle" (*La Pensée allemande,* p. 77).

[3] "'Celui qui ne parle pas' [the name they have given to Velu] avait mieux compris que ceux qui raisonnent. Et n'agissant que selon son instinct, il prétendait retourner aux lieux où il avait été aimé" (EL, pp. 215-216).

> Sa qualité dominante, c'était du ressort, et l'idée venait tout de suite d'un de ces poneys dont l'étymologie signifie jeune drôle, mais qui tiennent cependant un si joli quant à soi et font voir, avec beaucoup de piaffe, la plus seyante gravité, sous leur belle crinière peignée (EL pp. 25-26).

Such independence of personality, such maturity as Barrès endows her with in describing her as proud, obstinate, resilient, and gravely sensual are denied by the image which downgrades these human qualities to the instinctual behavioral traits of a thoroughbred animal. In fact, it is their common love of animals which brings André and Marina together in the first place. She tells André of her horses and her dog, and of her special preference for the little defenseless moles. Like children, animals are humble and pathetic in their trusting, often abused, dependence. In particular, the long-suffering fidelity of dogs makes them ideal objects of sentimentality. In Barrès' world, the role of women, children, and animals is to be beautiful and forlorn, and to invite the caresses of men. This debasement of women, and the way he diverts the sexual urge in these novels, do not make him very popular with today's readers. However, we should bear in mind that these are allegories and that he is carrying to an extreme, through simplification, stylization, and allegorical reduction, what was a common misogynistic tendency of the period.

A passage in *Mes Mémoires*,[4] in which Barrès recounts his earliest impression, testifies to the association of animality and childhood:

> Si j'essaye de me rappeler mon enfance et de repasser par les premières impressions de ma vie, elles me paraissent fort semblables à celles que j'ai pu observer chez un grand nombre de charmantes bêtes, des chiens surtout, avec lesquelles tout au long de ma vie j'ai vécu.

He remembers his first, purely material, sensations: the pleasures of food and drink. Since then, he writes, he has always been careful to feed animals. The origin of the special importance that he at-

---

[4] In the first volume of *Mes Cahiers*. My references are to the Plon edition.

tached to appetite as a sign of elementary desire can perhaps be detected in these reminiscences. These animal sensations marked him profoundly and continued to act on his mind all through his life. He tells us, for instance, that his childish impressions were the source of his sense of voluptuousness:

> Ai-je deux ans, trois ans, je me rappelle qu'on m'avait donné des étoupes de soie teintes de vert, de jaune, de violet, de toutes les couleurs, quel incroyable attrait, je les caressais. Il est difficile de rendre intelligible le battement de cœur, le bien-être de l'œil, la joie de possession qu'un enfant éprouve de ces petits trésors. C'est l'origine de la volupté.

The idea of the *petit trésor,* the infinitely valuable personal possession to which one clings, informs all his work. Bérénice is frequently described as a treasure, and it is in this spirit that Barrès elaborated and held to his intimate *truth.*

As for Rousseau, the child is truly the father of the man. In recalling these memories, Barrès traces a trait of his moral being to its first appearance, to its crystallization in the formative experience of childhood. Thus when he wishes to explain the attraction which foreign lands have for him, he remembers the days when, as a schoolboy, he used to dream in front of the windows of the *papeterie,* not on account of the photographs of actresses on display, but because he was fascinated by the faces of the politicians from all over Europe. They awoke in him a feeling of disquiet (*inquiétude* — strong feeling always has this anxious, irritant quality in Barrès' sensibility), a cosmopolitan urge to mingle with all the races of the world in which he found "quelque chose du mystérieux d'une étrangère excitante" (EL p. 164). Bérénice, Marina, La Pia, Mme Astine Aravian, and Marie Bashkirtsef (a real person this time)[5] were the forms this "étrangère excitante" assumed in the writings of the grown man.

The first anecdote that Marina recalls from her childhood, following immediately after the discussion on animals, illustrates the animality of her own sensual contact with the world, which is her principal attraction for André:

---

[5] See *Un Homme libre,* Chapter VIII and *Trois Stations de psychothérapie,* "La Légende d'une cosmopolite."

> Quand j'avais douze ans, disait-elle, j'amais, sitôt seule dans la campagne, à ôter mes chaussures et à enfoncer mes pieds nus dans la boue chaude. J'y passais des heures, et cela me donnait dans tout le corps un frisson de plaisir (p. 35).

The particularity of animals, children, and young women is their ability to experience directly, and with the greatest intensity, this *frisson*. It is the elemental thrilling of the senses to their naked contact with the world. The "Bonhomme Système" evokes the charming sensuality of women in terms that aptly describe the allegorical figures: "Roses écloses du matin..., les jeunes amantes ont de l'appétit, une âme amusante à fleur de peau" (SB p. 79). This epidermic response to life is constantly held up as an essential value by Barrès. In *Un Amateur d'âmes,* Delrio explains the special significance that he accords to the memory he has of himself as a child:

> Celui-là, pensait-il, n'avait encore rien ajouté à sa nature sincère. A fleur de peau, je laissais voir alors cette part essentielle que je ne puis plus retrouver en moi et sur laquelle il faut agir pour émouvoir profondément un être (SVM p. 34).

This unreflecting thrill of the nerve ends is not an end in itself, however, but it is the necessary beginning of all true knowledge. The task of the egotist, armed with his method, is to seize these *frissons* and bring them into consciousness: "Nous possédons là un don bien rare de noter les modifications de notre moi, avant que les frissons se soient effacés sur notre épiderme" (HL p. 13). The *frisson* is the point where body and soul meet, a reaction rooted in the nerve ends and reverberating through the conscious Self. It is of particular significance to Barrès, recurring time and time again in his writing to indicate the impingement of the world upon the Self. "Je veux accueillir tous les frissons de l'univers, je m'amuserai de tous mes nerfs" (HL p. 22). "Mon bonheur sera de me contempler agité de tous les frissons, et d'en être insatiable" (HL p. 41). The dilettante, the descendant of Baudelaire, and the contemporary of the decadents, is hungry to experience the most varied and subtle of these sensations. The problem for the decadent esthete was to find nourishment for an overrefined sensibility constantly threatened by the rapid blunting of its capacity for feeling. The originality of Barrès, in his search for stimulation in unusual directions, was undoubtedly his recourse to puerility and banal sentimentality allied to the most extravagant flights of voluptuous ecstasy.

The moralist, the seeker of energy, attaches himself to these *frissons* as guideposts along the way to self-knowledge and authentic moral engagement in the world. Philippe talks of the *frisson* which he feels when he reads the works of Benjamin Constant and Sainte-Beuve, and he explains how this leads him to a new awareness of some unknown part of his soul (HL p. 68). Later he says of Lorraine: "Mais qu'il est obscur,[6] indéchiffrable, le frisson qui nous attire vers cette vieille poussière de nos ancêtres!" (HL p. 105). Nevertheless, he does succeed in deciphering the lesson of his ancestors. The emotion is made to reveal the moral truth that it "signifies." The shiver of recognition, at the junction of body and mind, is the bridge between emotion and moral truth.

His soul is a "maîtresse frissonnante" (HL p. 89) and its allegorical projections have the role of reaping in the world a rich harvest of sensations, while Philippe-Barrès reaps the essence of these sensations: their moral abstraction. Bérénice is quite unable to understand the meaning of her own experience, but Philippe is there to transform it into thought.

> A petits pas nous rentrions à Rosemonde; elle n'avait pas de fleurs dans ses mains, et moi, de notre course, je ne rapportais non plus aucune notion. Mais au sang de ses veines s'était mêlé plus de soleil, plus de sel marin, plus du parfum des fleurs, et en moi s'était rafraîchi l'instinct, la force vive qui produit les hommes (pp. 113-14).

Bérénice absorbs the sensations that abound in the physical world, while Philippe, detached and reflective, absorbs their significance: the great lesson of the Unconscious.

Barrès' taste for "humiliated beauty," when carried just a little further, easily becomes a taste for mutilated beauty. Philippe

---

[6] *Obscur* — a favorite word in Barrès' vocabulary, expressing the idea of fertile profundity, of invisible, yet infallible, forces at work in nature and in history.

delights in the "beauté piétinée" of Bérénice (p. 23) and he regrets that she does not have some physical infirmity to which he could attach his feelings of pity. Failing this, he dwells on her "moral misery" (pp. 52-53). In the realm of art, he is particularly drawn to the mutilated statues of two sensuous dancers (p. 46). The masterpieces of 15th Century Franco-Flemish art (p. 27) among which Bérénice grew up and which influenced her vision of the world so much are described as "ces beautés finissantes" (p. 30). There is a special attraction for Barrès in the spectacle of beauty which is just on the point of expiring. He is fascinated by the art of civilizations which have disappeared, because the flowering of beauty is accompanied, in the mind of the spectator, by the imminence of death. The awareness of the presence of death at the source of pleasure irritates the sensibility and raises it to a new level of voluptuous intensity. Philippe's feeling for Bérénice is never stronger than when he is aware of what a transient thing life is. He dreams of protecting her against death, or, at least, of enjoying her ephemeral moment of beauty in one time-conquering sensation (p. 52).

Barrès' sentimental taste in pitiful, humiliated, and mediocre objects reveals a certain sado-masochism. Already in *Un Homme libre*, Philippe had observed that suffering and the pity it aroused was a superior form of love. I have shown how, in *L'Ennemi des lois*, pity becomes the guide to a fecund moral concern for the well-being of humanity, as André learns from Marina "what sensual pleasure there is in loving those that suffer" (p. 201). In the same way, Philippe is attracted to Bérénice because of her sufferings. She has lost the man she loved, and Philippe, participating vicariously in her emotions, is able himself to experience love "in the form of suffering." He describes his attachment to her as not exactly love or friendship, but rather as "un besoin extrême de douceur et de pleurs" (JB p. 44). Barrès himself admitted that this extreme sentimentality bordered on sadism: "C'est un sadisme, le besoin de voir des pleurs dans les yeux amoureux, d'énerver, de créer la plus intense sensibilité."[7] Philippe sums up the peculiar fascination that Bérénice has for him in this way: "Si j'ai tant aimé ma petite amie, c'est qu'elle était pour moi une

---

[7] *Mes Cahiers*, Plon, IV, 163.

chose d'amertume. Mon inclination ne sera jamais sincère qu'envers ceux de qui la beauté fut humiliée: souvenirs décriés, enfants froissés, sentiments offensés" (pp. 43-44). The inclination expressed here by Philippe is a fundamental trait of Barrès' sensibility. It is this penchant that determines not only his creation of Bérénice and Marina, but also of Astiné and Colette Baudoche, just as it marks his attitude to Lorraine and his choice of the subject in *La Colline inspirée*. The characteristic tone of so much of his work is created by the melancholy regret and exalted pathos which humiliated objects inspire in him. The lucid consciousness of his own existence is most strongly felt when it is generated by the image of oppression. The Barbarian is a structural necessity in the universe of his imagination.

The feeling of pity, devoid of the consuming passion that love arouses, does not absorb the Self in its object, but is constantly reflected back on the egotist in the form of heightened mental excitement. Pity is at once a sensual and moral attraction towards its object, but its sensuality is not materialized in physical possession. The caress is the limit of its physical contact, and consolation is its primary mode of expression. In fact, consoling is a form of moral caress: "C'est qu'il n'est pas de caresse plus tendre que de consoler" (JB p. 53). The superiority of pity over love for Barrès' heroes is precisely this interiorization of sensuality which quickens the moral awareness and increases the lucidity of consciousness to the point at which it begins to penetrate the world in the form of understanding. The moral lesson which Bérénice embodies is vivified by the transfer of the sensuality which she inspires in Philippe to his intellectual and political preoccupations. Where others had sought the touch of her body, Philippe seeks to caress the essence of her beauty: "Comme elle était habituée à faire voir son jeune corps sans voiles, elle laissa aussi mes mains se promener sur son âme passionnée" (JB p. 100). The image of his hands caressing her soul expresses this transfer of sensuality to the moral sphere.

In *Un Amateur d'âmes,* the sexual pleasure contained in the act of consoling attains a higher degree of intensity than the sexual act itself, and perhaps for this reason the accumulated and frustrated sensuality is redirected into sadism. As Delrio holds Simone in a passionate "brotherly" embrace, he feels a pleasure even stronger than that which their father had known when he conceived her. Thus Bérénice, Marina, and La Pia are presented as victims, poor unfortunate creatures whose role in life is to suffer.[8] They have been hurt first of all by existence — *froissé* is the adjective Barrès often uses to describe this painful contact with a cruel world. They are victims, too, of the men whose objects they become. Philippe is indirectly the cause of Bérénice's death, when he forces her to marry Charles Martin. Already suffering at the loss of her lover, M. de Transe, she withers away in the proximity of this Barbarian. Philippe, of course, is well aware of the hurt he causes, and this only adds to the poignancy of his later regret. Delrio, by deliberately arousing the exquisite hypersensitivity of La Pia, so troubles her that she commits suicide.[9] Although Marina survives, André sacrifices her devotion and inflicts considerable pain upon her when he marries Claire. Even though the suffering they cause is unintentional, each derives a sadistic pleasure from the spectacle of pain. When Philippe has finished telling Simon about his "experiments" with Bérénice, he observes that his story has had the same effect on his friend as if someone had crushed a dog's paw right under his eyes (p. 1333). The transition from moral to real physical pain is metaphorical here, but in *Un Amateur d'âmes* it is completed literally. Delrio's excitement reaches a paroxysm as La Pia lies in agony on her death-bed: "Depuis ton éclatante et surprenante décision, combien je t'aime ainsi sanglante! et que je te désire sous ce pâle et sous ce rouge de la mort!" (p. 72).

It is the Escurial which awakens Delrio to this voluptuousness of death. He is overwhelmed by the "catholic empire of suffering" and he feels that nothing stirs the depths of our consciousness so much as the beauty of the leper-hospital (p. 49)! And beyond death, decomposition itself is a source of morbid pleasure. Some

---

[8] Jacques Vier says of Bérénice: "A son propos, s'accomplit en lui un mélange singulier de bourreau et de victime, la satisfaction d'opprimer, les délices de souffrir" ("Barrès et le culte du moi," p. 47).

[9] Delrio carries this sadism to greater lengths than either Philippe or André. He even obliges Simone to wear a kind of hair shirt: "Par une bizarrerie d'imagination, il l'avait priée de ne porter comme lingerie que de rudes et grossières toiles; il lui plaisait que cette façon de cilice atténué le liât constamment, dans l'esprit de la jeune fille, à une gêne d'ordre si intime" (p. 38).

withered magnolias are the occasion of some strangely macabre imagery which prefigures the tragedy that is to come:

> Les pulpes blanches des larges fleurs qu'ils emportaient se tachèrent de mort. La souffrance fit éclore en les violentant quelques corolles. Ces masses somptueuses ainsi défaites et carnées donnaient la plus triste impression d'accablement et de désastre (SVM pp. 61-62).

In *L'Ennemi des lois,* when André announces the news that Velu has run away, he and Marina arrive in imagination at a similar "leprous beauty." Quite beside herself with grief, Marina whispers: "Oh André, I wish you were dead" (p. 223). He fully understands this "pensée d'amour"! Nevertheless she goes on to explain·her meaning; if he were dead, she would only have to cherish the image she had of him in memory, without fearing the flow of time. We recognize the familiar theme that absolute possession is only possible in memory when death has destroyed the ephemeral present. These thoughts of death and possession trigger a vision of sadistic intensity as each imagines the other as a corpse and evokes the "abominable ceremonies" of death (p. 224). They find, however, that Velu has been taken to the vivisectionist's. The laboratory and the garden around it are described as an idyllic place, but the calm beauty of the setting is marred by a "strong smell of decomposition" (p. 230).

In all these cases — the death of Bérénice and of La Pia, and the episode of Velu's disappearance — it is pity rather than sexual desire which occasions the rising notes of sadistic intensity. The scene of Velu's flight is a veritable orgy of pity: "La pitié les avait envahis l'un et l'autre, elle et lui sur le Velu, chacun d'eux sur l'autre et chacun sur soi-même" (p. 219). When the dog's flight is announced, Claire, recognizing the bond which unites André and Marina, overcomes her rational tendencies and obeys the call of her heart: "Courez, dit-elle, chez votre amie" (p. 216). She realizes that she cannot occupy the place in André's heart that Marina does, because only by making him unhappy could she have become as precious to him as Marina: "Il vous faut les nerfs brisés pour que vous ne soyez pas atone. C'était certain que vous courriez là où vous pouvez souffrir" (pp. 218-219). "Nerfs brisés" and "courir" are favorite expressions of Barrès'. The nerves stretched to breaking point translate the almost unhealthy quality of exacerbated feeling, while the desire to run conveys the urgency with which he cultivates the thrill of being moved. His heroes are usually incapable of passionate attachment to any creature or to any thing outside themselves. Love is impossible. But, on the other hand, they constantly search out occasions to experience emotion vicariously by way of a pity which involves the spectator without really breaking down the distance which sets him apart.

Related to Barrès' taste for suffering and mutilation is his preference for tainted objects. The allegorical creatures of his sensuality are consistently represented as impure. There is a keen pleasure in the convergence of innocence and corruption; it is the point at which sentimentality can be joined to sensuality. Indeed it is also the point at which purity becomes a source of sensuality while, at the same time, acting as a check to render it inoperative. Philippe is sensually drawn to Bérénice, but the sentimental emotion aroused by her childlike innocence stops short of any desire for sexual possession. The child prostitute in whom the corruption of the body is paralleled by the virgin candor of the soul is an ideal figure. The young girl in *Sous l'œil des barbares* is cast in very much these terms, as is the "Object" in *Un Homme libre*. Bérénice is a "petite libertine" (p. 19) who has been subjected to the vulgar embrace of many men, but at the same time she has retained the purity of her childhood. Marina, too, is described as being without moral scruples ("sans freins moraux" [EL p. 83]): she had deliberately used her charms to try to seduce men when she was still a girl. In the novel, she is living alone as a courtesan in a typical late nineteenth century *demi-monde* setting. Marina belongs to that other category of female phantasies in Barrès' works, of which the Oriental Amaryllis in *Sous l'œil des barbares* is the first example. But the sensuality of these creatures is once again an unfulfilled promise, as gratuitous as the accoutrements of luxury which surround them. It is not sexual desire that attracts André to Marina; her voluptuousness remains quite sterile, an ornamentation to the delights of pity.

The same aura of innocent corruption surrounds Simone in *Un Amateur d'âmes*. She is described as "cette petite fille pure" (SVM p. 41), but her purity is tarnished by a hereditary stain.

She is an illegitimate child, "l'enfant d'(un) péché" (p. 36). Under an appearance of melancholic and icy perfection, there beats a heart "capable of the most beautiful disorders" (p. 36). The absence of any sexual contact, which has been observed as one of the characteristics of sensuality in Barrès' phantasies, is intensified in this story by the added barrier of incest. Not only does her childlike innocence place Simone beyond the physical fulfillment of desire, but the fact that she is Delrio's sister multiplies the enervating accumulation of unreleased sensuality. In Barrès' universe, the most intense sensuality that a voluptuous mistress can arouse in her lover is projected onto a creature who is not to be possessed. The accumulated tension is directed inwards.

Often a religious dimension increases the erotic tension between innocence and impurity, widening the gap and heightening the excitement. The contrast is now between sin and piety. Simone is the child of a sin, and her incestuous attachment to her brother is a corruption, but she is first presented to the reader as a religious little soul. She is, after all, also called La Pia. To describe the quality of Bérénice's soul, Philippe can find no better term than "religious": "Tu es macérée de douceur, la qualité religieuse de ton cœur est exquise" (JB p. 164). The verb *macérer* and the adjective *exquis* convey the strongly sensual nature of Barrès' religiosity; the verb in particular, with its overtones of "mortification" suggests a sensuality which is felt almost as a wound. The contrast between sin and saintliness is thus ideal: "Pitoyable et fanée de péchés, elle avait un nimbe lumineux où s'éclairait ma conscience" (pp. 199-200). "Fanée de péchés" — thus Philippe finds in the beloved object, whose religious purity and almost mystical luminosity are a spiritual guide to his soul,[10] that "blemish" which is for him a crowning perfection.

For Barrès, the religious emotion itself is a certain voluptuous fullness of the soul, an essentially feminine melting of the senses, so that the image of a young woman in adoration before the Virgin Mary is its most appropriate expression. And how much

---

[10] Philippe describes the land around Aigues-Mortes, spiritualized by the presence of Bérénice and her animals, as a "fecund chapel of meditation." Bérénice herself is the object of what is almost a "religious" cult; she is described by Philippe as his "altar" and his "cloister" (p. 170).

more delicious if that young woman is degraded by sin! One of the first images in *Un Homme libre* to identify the cult of the Self with the rites of Catholicism establishes this fundamental association of religious emotion and femininity:

> L'amour de Dieu soulevait ma poitrine.
> Je dis Dieu, car de l'éclosion confuse qui se fit alors en mon imagination, rien n'approche autant que l'ardeur d'une jeune femme, chercheuse et comblée, lasse du monde qu'elle ne saurait quitter et qui, dévote, s'agenouille en vous invoquant, Marie Vierge et Christ Dieu (p. 17).

What interests Barrès is the peculiar flavor of her devotion, its psychological origin in her vague dissatisfaction and world-weariness. The image calls to mind Amaryllis in Chapter III of *Sous l'œil des barbares,* whose yearning for an ideal brought about her conversion to a religion in which there was a place for a sensual courtesan. He was particularly touched by the fact that Christianity was the religion of sinners and prostitutes. He was drawn to the *tableau* of the young and beautiful creature, tainted by the most attractive of sins, at the feet of Christ and his Virgin Mother. Mary Madeleine was an archetypal figure in his phantasies.[11]

The allegorical "universe" that Barrès creates as the full flowering of the cult of the Self, in *Le Jardin de Bérénice, L'Ennemi des lois* and *Du sang, de la volupté et de la mort,* is the garden in which all his phantasies, *rêveries,* and romantic imaginations take root and grow to fruition. Sensuality, morbidity, banal sentimentality, the various endeavors of a late romantic sensibility to maintain a fever pitch of emotional fullness in a world threatened by the constant destruction of feeling, are projected around his cherished allegories. They are exteriorized; a distance is established between the egotist and his romantic tendencies

---

[11] Already in his analysis of the "religious" dimension of the modern sensibility, *à propos* of Baudelaire, Barrès had evoked this kind of image: "Les courtisanes de jadis, les femmes que nous chérissons pour le parfum qui demeure d'elles, ces orientales inquiètes qui descendirent des lits d'amour pour marcher au Christ rédempteur et dont les chairs caressées, s'étant crispées dans toutes les angoisses de la chair, s'abandonnèrent au pied de celui-ci qui apaise" (*Les Taches d'encre,* p. 400).

which might otherwise have consumed him. He can be moved and watch himself being moved; he can at once enjoy and analyze his sensations. Romanticism is rationalized, cultivated for the lessons it can give. Many of the themes that Philippe projects onto Bérénice are traditionally romantic: she broods in melancholy solitude over a lost lover; from her nostalgia for the past she constructs her present happiness and unconsciously creates, from her regret, an ideal of happiness far superior to the reality she had briefly known. Philippe, who is at all times the lucid observer can both indulge in the emotions and classify them intellectually, be involved and detached at the same time. Philippe's attitude to Bérénice exactly reflects Barrès' attitude to his own sensibility: he studies it with passionate and lucid curiosity: "Nous la regardions, comme font trois amateurs autour de la chrysalide où se débat ils ne savent quel papillon" (JB p. 24). The insects' flight in *Sous l'œil des barbares* was the symbol of the frivolity and the absolute futility of the *Amie,* the allegory of his sensual self. Yet it was she who served as the young man's guide to self-awareness. If the garden is Philippe's frivolous garden of delights, it is also a fertile place where the vital principle which he discovers at the heart of his emotions, incarnate in Bérénice, can take root and break through the sterility of this endless adornment of the Self. Through the intermediary of allegory, the intensity of emotion is transformed into creative moral energy.

Chapter V

THE ANALOGICAL UNIVERSE

Apart from the earlier chapters of *Sous l'œil des barbares*, where the decor is a symbolist dream landscape, the "universe" is constructed from observations of the real world. Lorraine, Southern France, Spain, Italy, and Germany provide the background to Barrès' novels. However, they clearly cannot be described as realistic. Rather there is an imaginative reconstruction of the elements into an abstract pattern which functions allegorically. Philippe says of the *tour Constance:* "En vérité, ce nom de Constance n'est-il pas tel qu'on l'eût choisi, dans une carte idéologique à la façon des cartes du Tendre...?" (JB p. 87). The allegorical nature of his descriptions is defined precisely by this "ideological" quality.

The descriptions of landscapes and cities, the reflections on art, the evocations of historical personages and events, all have a moral significance directly related to the themes of these works. They do not stand on their own as existing objectively, but serve as material illustrations of the same message that is revealed by the feminine projections of Barrès' soul. The process by which the given reality of the outside world is assimilated to the "universe" is one of analogy, a drawing-in of certain elements of reality selected in view of their moral resemblance to the Self or of their relevance to its intellectual and moral inquiry. The choice of those elements is governed by the criterion of their "usefulness." Thus, Barrès asks himself how he can "utilize" Athens (*Voyage de Sparte,* p. 49), and Philippe calls Venice "this abstract city, built for my personal use" (HL p. 179).

The term "analogy" is preferable to "correspondences," suggested by one critic, to designate this assimilation of the real world to the Self. Bernhard Baur refers to Baudelaire and Rimbaud to justify his choice of the latter term.[1] However, analogy is the word used very often by Barrès himself to describe his technique, and correspondences bring to mind a form of poetic imagery which is quite absent from his works. Baudelairian and Symbolist correspondences are suggestive, mysterious, profoundly sensual, while Barrès' analogies are intellectually constructed and quite explicit. The function of analogy is to equate on a more literal plane than simile or metaphor. He is seeking to establish a systematic and permanent system of relationships rather than a sudden illuminating similarity.

When he compares Bérénice to a young birch-tree (p. 96), the image has a special resonance in view of the fact she is consistently represented as the embodiment of the life-force in whom the sap of the universe is flowing. Images of this kind are functional.[2] Their purpose is not just to embellish the text, but to reinforce the thematic relationships within it. When Venice is compared to "une dormeuse parée" in *L'Ennemi des lois* (p. 107), the image itself is relevant to the analogical association of the city and the voluptuous Marina. The process is quite similar to the reduction of certain notions such as taste and appetite: the effect is to literalize the imagery — as when Barrès writes that the Bavarian socialists, in their demands for reform, feel the same anguish as the dog Velu confronted by a steaming plate of food that he is forbidden to touch (EL p. 157). The simile merely confirms the fundamental identification of socialism and hunger that has been created by the analogical anecdotes. The angle of difference is reduced. When Barrès describes Bérénice as a birch-tree, he is not thinking so much of the spectacle of the tree as of the idea it embodies. The relation is logical rather than imaginative.

---

[1] *Versuch über Inhalt, Motive, Stil in "Le Culte du moi" von Maurice Barrès*, Strasburg, Heitz, 1937, p. 118.

[2] See Jean Ricardou's article on the "functional" or "structural" use of imagery in literature: "Expression et fonctionnement," *Tel Quel*, Vol. 24 (Winter, 1966). Ricardou makes a distinction between the expressive and the functional image. The latter must be understood not just in the immediate context but within the total meaning of the text.

Analogies serve, then, to relate the different parts of the "universe" to each other. In *Le Jardin de Bérénice,* the largest number of these analogies are centered around Bérénice; and, in fact, we can see that she is *constructed* piece by piece out of the impressions that Barrès received when he visited the region of Arles and Aigues-Mortes. The great originality of this novel is the way in which a highly stylized, complex, and dynamic allegorical form is given to the quite ordinary impressions that any sensitive man might enjoy on visiting Southern France. She is first of all related to the museum in which Philippe finds the same "charme délicat et misérable" (p. 26), the same fragile beauty that had attracted him to her. She has the "strange delicacy" of 15th Century Burgundian art, touching and somehow pathetic in its neglected glory. Bérénice is indeed "l'âme projetée" (p. 36) of the museum. Philippe links the crumbling monuments of Arles to his image of Bérénice who has suffered and is to die at the hands of the Barbarians. Aigues-Mortes, lost among its memories and unchangingly faithful to its past, is analogous to the noble melancholy of the young woman who lives for her memories of M. de Transe. Both lead Philippe to an awareness of deep hereditary sentiments (p. 90). In the same way, the barren landscape with its dry expanses and its insalubrious salt marshes which is so intimately linked with the melancholy Bérénice: "ce pays lunaire plein de rêves immenses et de tristesses résignées," is in perfect harmony with Philippe's soul in its alternating moods of sterility and feverish *rêverie.* These analogies serve to assimilate certain aspects of the outside world to Bérénice and hence to Barrès' own allegorized soul. Thus the world is the mirror of the Self. Sainte-Beuve and Benjamin Constant "ne valent que comme miroirs grossissants pour certains détails de [son] âme" (HL p. 141); Lorraine is "a more powerful mirror than any of the analysts in whom [he] observed [himself]" (p. 131); in Venice Philippe says: "J'obtins une image infiniment noble où je me mirai avec délice dans ma chambre solitaire et fraîche... Voici donc que je contemplais mes émotions!" (HL p. 183). By the selective technique of analogy, he admires his own embellished image in the world around him, while at the same time he can learn from what he finds.

The museum in which Bérénice grows up surrounded by paintings, statues, and tapestries, is an image of the world in its diversity and in its unity. Some of the images it contains are incomprehensible to her, but she is intuitively aware that they are charged with meaning. They are signs which instruct and guide her, forming her character in their own likeness as she contemplates their mysterious complexity and strange beauty. For Barrès, too, the world is a system of signs, a rebus to be deciphered and interpreted (p. 34) so that reality can be made to *speak,* to reveal its inner significance. It is a potential source of education for him, just as the museum is for Bérénice.

Yet if the world is seen as a "vast spectacle," as a book laid open to the eyes of the observer, the analogy of the museum also suggests that reality must be observed in a limited and selective perspective. The tapestries and paintings represent the world in its multiplicity, but they also represent it as a simplification. The tapestry which occupies a place of honor in the museum (pp. 30-31) is an image of the novel itself, of the allegorical garden in which Bérénice moves among her animals. It is an image, too, of the artificial "universe" in which the chaos of phenomena has been selectively recreated by the Self. Just as the details of a tapestry are selected for their allegorical appropriateness and arranged in view of an esthetic effect, so the elements of the "universe" are organized as a thematic harmony. Like the tapestry, the "universe" is at once moving, beautiful, and instructive. The reality it portrays is stylized and flat. Its complexity is in the subtle relations exposed on the surface of the material, in the repetition of motifs and in the absence of relief. It is two-dimensional; a flower, an animal, a human figure are all on the same plane and have equal value.[3]

The process by which the egotist can determine what is already analogous to his own Self amidst the multiplicity of phenomena

---

[3] Albert Thibaudet has remarked on this resemblance of the novel to a medieval allegory: "Moréas y retrouvait la manière de conter de nos fabliaux, ce en quoi il se trompe; mais la subtilité, la complexité et la vie des allégories y rappellent le *Roman de la rose.* Nous sommes bien dans le musée du roi René. Si la rose allégorisait l'amour, Bérénice allégorise le Moi au moment où, comme une chaîne de montagnes sous le couchant, il va prendre avant de s'éteindre toute sa gamme de nuances et de pierreries, — Le Moi dans tout son beau jardin d'émotions, sa réceptivité féminine" (*La Vie de Maurice Barrès,* Vol. II of *Trente ans de vie française,* Gallimard, 1921, p. 153).

is one of unconscious identification. On the very first page of *Le Jardin de Bérénice,* Barrès explains that deep inside us there are invisible "powers" which are not revealed as exterior acts:

> Elles font sur notre âme de petites taches, cachées dans une ombre presque absolue, mais insensiblement autour de ce noyau viennent se cristalliser tout ce que la vie nous fournit de sentiments analogues (p. 1).

An inner force, an essential inclination which might be called our true nature or our fundamental sensibility, carries out an intuitive selection among the data of experience. These analogies are, then the unconscious creation of the Self and they await the moment of illumination to reveal themselves, as they do for Philippe as he meditates on the *Tour Constance:* "Dans cette solitude... les analogies les plus cachées apparaissaient à mon esprit" (JB p. 85). The world may be a rebus for Barrès, but its signs speak to him only of himself. The egotist interrogates the world in which the meaning of his own Self is hidden.

Le Voyage de Sparte provides an explicit statement of this selective vision which can only penetrate what is assimilable to his own sensibility. Barrès describes the feeling of disappointment which he experienced upon his arrival in Greece. He had expected to be intensely moved by that country which his illustrious predecessors, Byron, Chateaubriand, Lamartine, Renan, and Taine had celebrated, but he found no point of contact with the beauty before his eyes. I cannot make use of any beauty, he says, unless I can establish a communication between my heart and its heart (p. 48):

> Il faudrait qu'en me repliant sur moi-même je trouvasse dans mon âme des réalités morales, des besoins et des émotions, analogues à celles qui s'expriment par ces statues, par ces architectures et par ces paysages grecs (p. 49).[4]

---

[4] Also in *Le Voyage de Sparte,* he writes: "Je cherchais d'abord, dans Athènes, des objets analogues à ceux qui, dans d'autres pays, m'avaient donné du bonheur" (p. 37). In his later works, there is an unwillingness or inability to be moved to discover new points of similarity between his soul and the places he visited.

As Barrès tells his readers time and time again, he is not receptive to the physical beauty or the external fascination of the world. His vision is of the ideological, or moral, reality which underlies phenomena. His poetic response to the world is intellectual and not visual: "La beauté du dehors jamais ne m'émut vraiment. Les plus beaux spectacles ne me sont que des tableaux psychologiques" (HL p. 174). The chapter from which this famous observation is taken describes Philippe's visit to Venice, after the termination of his spiritual retreat in Saint-Germain. He is overwhelmed by the city, but he feels that he cannot absorb this experience in the moment of enjoying it. His real possession of the city comes later; he waits impatiently for the day when he will have finished seeing everything, because then he will be able to close his eyes and transform what he has seen into the matter of thought ("faire des pensées enfin avec ces choses que j'avais frolées" p. 174). A little later he explains that his "ideologist's curiosity" leads him to consider all these beautiful forms and tangible splendors as symbols of the intangible beauty of ideas.[5]

Although one can undoubtedly detect a certain influence of the ideas in vogue in the late eighties, Barrès is not really very close to the theories of Symbolism in these declarations. When he uses the word "ideas," he means quite literally "thoughts," and not mystical Ideas or Essences. These symbols are not the esthetic equivalents of a mysterious Other World beyond this one, but simply the concrete features of the world which are the raw materials of his reflections. It is true that he is interested in essences and not in outward appearances, but the essence of a thing is not its metaphysical being which art tries to reproduce imaginatively, but its moral significance in as much as it can become meaningful to the observer.

Similarly in *Colette Baudoche:* "Il est impossible d'aimer, voire de comprendre aucun objet si nous n'avons pas mêlé nos songes à sa réalité, établi un lien entre lui et notre vie. C'est peu d'avoir consciencieusement tourné autour d'une belle chose: l'essentiel c'est de sentir sa qualité morale et de participer du principe d'où elle est née" (p. 135).

[5] And similarly: "Cet ensemble d'un pittoresque provocant... nul voyageur qui ne le saisisse, mais l'esprit, la qualité morale de cette reine détrônée, voilà ce qu'il nous faut comprendre" (*Greco ou le secret de Tolède,* p. 82).

Similarly, in art, it is not the outer beauty which Barrès sets out to capture, but the inner form, the moral reality of which the work is the sign. Reflecting on the sculptures of Phidias in *Le Voyage de Sparte,* he refers to the "moral model," the "living thought" which the artist bore in his heart (pp. 65-66). Barrès seeks to decipher the moral vision which the artist has objectified in his work. He admits that he is neither a sculptor nor a connoisseur of plastic beauty, but he does feel himself qualified to understand statures as the "fixed expression of a certain sensibility" (p. 66).

It is this inner vision [6] which permits the egotist to isolate the spectacle, to relate it to himself, and to interpret the analogies it may contain with his soul. Outer beauty is not irrelevant, however, for it provides that first indispensable flood of emotion after which the eyes of the mind construct a permanent idea in which the inner beauty of the spectacle is abstracted from the ephemeral impression: "Je le dis, un instant des choses, si beau qu'on l'imagine, ne saurait guère m'intéresser" (HL p. 180). Just as the esthetic beauty of a work of art is only the visible sign of the "moral model" in which it is grounded, so the outside world in its concrete reality is only the emblem of its underlying meaning. The senses respond directly and intuitively to the world of phenomena in which they are rooted, and, in so doing, they establish the necessary communication between two moral beings: the Self and the being of the world.

The mode of this inner vision is meditation. When Philippe has completed his inspection of Venice, he shuts himself up in his room for the real task of uncovering the essence of the city ("L'Être de Venise" as one part of this chapter is subtitled). He proceeds to "eliminate" (p. 182) all that is superfluous in his first impressions until he discovers the point of connection between Venice and his own soul. [7] By this process of elimination and abstraction,

---

[6] "Heureux les yeux qui, fermés aux choses extérieures, ne contemplent plus que les intérieures" (HL, p. 177).
[7] Bernard Baur has analyzed this suppression or elimination of details in *Le Jardin de Bérénice,* particularly in the landscape descriptions. He observes how little local color there is and how much the landscape is dematerialized (*Inhalt, Motive, Stil,* pp. 133-35). He refers to some notes that Barrès had made for the description of Le Grau-du-Roi and shows

he forces the analogies, which were present but not manifest in his initial response, to stand out from the mass of irrelevancies. The meaning of Venice is suddenly clear, and the emotion it arouses is permanently fixed: Philippe realizes that it is not just its material appearance in any given moment of time, but the sum of all the successive moments through which it has passed since it came into existence. It is the symbol of the continuity of the spirit working through a distinctive human collectivity.

Barrès' "universe" is intensely humanified; his vision of the outside world is always of the witness it bears to the human soul. The role of meditation is to reflect upon the historical evolution of a city or a landscape so that the past will illuminate the meaning of the present. He evokes the history of Venice, comparing its development point by point with his own (HL pp. 185-191). His treatment of history is highly selective, with little regard for objectivity. He only dwells on the facts that reveal the fundamental human struggle for existence. Thus we learn that Venice was founded by a group of men, fiercely independent and proud of their freedom, who continually strove to resist all foreign intrusion — just as Philippe had rejected the Barbarians (p. 185).[8] Barrès is interested in individual historical figures only when their actions dramatically embody a stage in the general development of the collective soul. In his very similar meditation upon Lorraine, Philippe traces its development from its "birth" to its "death," celebrating in particular René II who gave such impetus to the young nation (pp. 98-100). It is significant that Barrès regards the history of a nation in terms of the human life-cycle of birth, growth, maturity, and decline.

In history's gallery of great men, he selects those who strike a sympathetic note in harmony with his own soul. His portrait of Disraeli in *L'Ennemi des lois* is a remarkable likeness to the young Barrès: "Disraeli se composait de la vie une imagination

---

that in the novel most of the particular details have vanished: "Die übrigen scharf gesehenen Einzelheiten (diese angeführten gleich vielen anderen) werden im Roman ausgeschaltet, damit nichts ablenke vom gewollten Eindruck der grossen Einfachheit, Eintönigkeit, Leere und 'Geistigkeit' der Landschaft" (*Inhalt*, p. 134).

[8] Barrès even compares the early days of Venice to his own "mortified childhood" (pp. 185-86).

sensuelle et chimérique" (p. 141). He is passionate and disinterested at the same time, he has a taste for the artificial and an ability to carry several different lives to esthetic perfection at the same time (p. 142). This is the language with which Barrès characterizes the superior dilettantism of Philippe in *Un Homme libre*. The last part of chapter IV in *L'Ennemi des lois* is entitled "Voyage idéologique aux châteaux de Louis II." The mad prince is described as a late Romantic or Symbolist hero striving to give a permanent form to his dream by the construction of his fantastic and useless castles. He takes Wagner as his spiritual guide, and Barrès likens his endeavor to a voyage out of this world with Parsifal. Louis II represents "a perfect problem of ethics" (p. 180): "Il nous fait toucher l'antinomie irréductible d'un rêve avec sa réalisation" (p. 180). Again Barrès uses the characteristic language of his own egotism to portray the prince — "se créer une vie wagnérienne" (p. 195); "erreurs de méthode" (p. 195); des idéals qu'il se composait" (pp. 195-196); "ne se plaire que dans la tristesse" (p. 185); "il affirmait son moi contre son entourage" (p. 178). How far Barrès will go in using a historical figure as a receptacle for his own categories is revealed in the account of the prince's suicide. When he drags down into the water with him that Doctor Gudden who has been assigned to control the excesses of his madness, Barrès interprets his act as one of vengeance against a barbarian who has been attempting to impose a foreign "rule of life" (p. 194) upon him. History, like everything else in the outside world, is exemplary.

The historical information which Barrès uses is never more precise than what one can find in tourist guidebooks or museum catalogues.[9] Specific details are anecdotal, designed to dramatize a general truth from a particular situation. The "truth" of history lies in the beauty of the gesture, in the universality of the moral drama, and in the pathos of its tragedies. History is the museum of the human soul, full of moving and morally instructive *tableaux*, just as the presently existing world is a great museum for this singular connoisseur. His travels are symptomatic of his attitude.

---

[9] Before his trip to Italy, Philippe is seen thumbing through the Baedeker guides (HL, p. 147).

Alone [10] and detached from the existential reality of the places he visited, guidebook in hand, [11] he passed before the great monuments of human achievement in search of that thrill of emotion which would illuminate his own soul and relate it to the world. The many journeys that he made throughout his life were conducted very much in the spirit of the young man in *Sous l'œil des barbares* cynically planning the future organization of his life:

> Chaque année, de rapides voyages de trente jours me mèneraient à Venise pour ennoblir mon type, à Dresde pour rêver devant ses peintures et ses musiques, au Vatican et à Berlin pour que leurs antiques précisent mes rêves (p. 270).

As we have seen, museums have quite literally an important place in Barrès' works, for it was often to painting and sculpture that he turned to discover the moral significance of what he saw on his travels. In his meditations upon Venice and Lorraine, the works of the great artist appear on the same plane as historical data. Art and history are really identical for him, since both testify to the same moral reality. They both embody, with the same poetic truth, the drama of the collective soul, its struggles, its fears, its aspirations, and its achievement. The evocation of Venice is based almost exclusively on the reflections of its development in the works of the great masters, Titian, Tintoretto, Veronese, Tiepolo

---

[10] In reality, as Jérôme and Jean Tharaud observe, Barrès hated physical solitude, although in spirit he was a profoundly solitary man: "Cet homme que si souvent parlait de solitude, et qui était bien en effet un esprit solitaire, détestait être seul. Il lui fallait toujours un compagnon de promenade" (*Mes Années chez Barrès*, Plon, 1928, p. 158).

[11] Jacques Vier suggests that Barrès was influenced by Taine's *Voyage en Italie* ("Barrès et le culte du moi," p. 26). He points out that he never went to Venice without a copy of Taine's book — "comme le plus précieux des Baedeker" (p. 33).

Certainly Barrès took his travels seriously as a "man of letters" if not as a scientist or historian. He seems to have experienced something of the vertigo which Taine felt among the endless succession of "things to be seen": "On voit passer devant soi des milliers et encore des milliers d'objets; tout cela au retour s'agite dans la tête: comment retirer de ce chaos quelque impression dominante, quelque vue d'ensemble" (*Voyage en Italie*, Hachette, 1910, Vol. I, 57). Barrès strives to isolate the "dominant impression," the "general view," but the elaborately decorative and impressionistic style of Taine is altogether absent from his work.

(pp. 186-191). Great works of art are the visible signs which mark a nation's progress through time.

The opening chapter of *La Colline inspirée*, "Il est des lieux où souffle l'esprit," provides the best definition of the quality that Barrès seeks in the landscapes he describes: "Il est des lieux qui tirent l'âme de sa léthargie, des lieux enveloppés, baignés de mystère, élus de toute éternité pour être le siège de l'émotion religieuse" (p. 1). Throughout the world there are a certain number of privileged places, "hauts lieux," [12] which speak to the soul and inspire a deep intensity of emotional fervor. They are places distinguished by a dramatic atmosphere of spirituality, places in which that quality of "soul" is concentrated and manifest to the eyes of the inner vision. Their inspirational power is such that they appear as a living presence imposing themselves on the sensibility of the onlooker. They are the shrines which accumulate and transmit the acquired wealth of the past. The adjective "haut," which Barrès uses in a wide range of contexts, conveys this notion of moral superiority. Although the sense is primarily of spiritual elevation, many of these privileged places do quite literally dominate the landscape around them. The hill of Sion in *La Colline inspirée* stands out like a promontory (p. 5), like "an altar raised up in the middle of the plateau" (p. 4). The landscape of Aigues-Mortes is seen from the ramparts of the old city and the *tour Constance*. Toledo stands majestically on its hill overlooking the Tagus and the Escurial dominates the rugged meseta for miles around.

They are characterized by an atmosphere of sadness, rugged desolation, or magnificent solitude. The Spanish landscape have a quality which Barrès calls "âpreté," a barrenness, a raw spiritual nakedness which grates on the nerves and fills the soul with a heroic and mystical elevation. The same *dénuement* is the secret of the attraction of Aigues-Mortes and the hill of Sion which rises up in wild and lonely contrast to the monotonous plain which surrounds it. The dramatic starkness of Aigues-Mortes and Spain gives way to the fog-enshrouded mystery, the primitive Celtic

---

[12] The influence of Renan can be felt behind Barrès' exalted meditations. See the "Prière sur l'Acropole" in *Souvenirs d'enfance et de jeunesse*.

gloom of Sion, but the emotion which they arouse is much the same.

Barrès finds in these landscapes a moral quality almost identical to that which he finds in the works of Pascal. He announces on the first page of *Un Amateur d'âmes,* in the chapter entitled "L'Exaltation dans la solitude," that anyone familiar with the Toledan landscape would have no need to read the *Pensées* or to see Da Vinci's *Pensieroso* in the Medici chapel: the sad, yet ardent Castillian scenery around Toledo would convey the same feeling as these works (SVM p. 31). The impression is of "energy" and "passion," of "vigor" and "mystery" (p. 32), a grave and somber ardor lifting the soul upwards to a perception of the infinite. The Jansenist fear and trembling have become an almost sensual *frisson* of mystical exaltation. Pascal's dramatization of human insignificance amid the abysses of space has become the voluptuous pleasure in the contemplation of death. The "leprous beauty" of the Escurial, which arouses in Delrio the "vertigo of the ascetic abyss" and awakens him to the "Catholic empire of suffering" is, Barrès tells us, exactly the spectacle Pascal would have evoked in one of his meditations (p. 49). He sees in Pascal a tortured, solitary soul, struggling heroically with his tragic vision, but more than recompensed by the magnificent exaltation that he received in return. The self-consciousness which the 19th Century introduced into all its attitudes turned every emotion into an object, somehow exterior to the individual, to be possessed and enjoyed as an intimate personal treasure. Any awareness, however anguished, even of death or damnation itself, carries an automatic compensation when its very intensity is a source of a more ecstatic self-possession. It is this shift in sensibility which permits Barrès to accommodate Pascal (and Catholicism in general) to the heart of his own vision:

> Peu m'importe le fond des doctrines! C'est l'élan que je goûte. Les ascètes d'Espagne ou de Port-Royal appelaient vivre pour l'éternité ce que nous appelons s'observer, comprendre le néant de la vie. Ces états élevés seraient-ils perdus aujourd'hui? (pp. 49-50). [13]

---

[13] See Jacques Mercanton, *Poésie et religion dans l'œuvre de Maurice Barrès,* Lausanne, 1940, pp. 211-217, for a discussion of Barrès' attach-

The "religious emotions" of *La Colline inspirée* is already present in these earlier landscape descriptions.

Barrès' landscapes objectify the drama within his soul between the opposing tendencies to mind-dissolving expansion and the austere concentration of his forces within himself, between the threat of infinite dispersion and the solidity of permanence.[14] There is always a tension which can be dramatized as a dialectical struggle between opposites. The dialogue is at the heart of his creative process. It is one of the fundamental techniques which generate the text around the central object of meditation. First of all, an emotional reaction which provides the point of departure — the mood of the place, a certain spiritual impression; then, in a second movement, the spiritualized landscape is assimilated by analogy to the themes of Barrès' own inner life. Different points or aspects of the scene are charged with a specific meaning until the initial, uniform impression has been clarified and strongly articulated around a simple opposition or tension. Then, in the final development of these constructive meditations, the entire structure is set in movement as it were, as Barrès begins to elaborate on the themes, to penetrate their meaning, and to draw out the lessons which they contain for his own self-perfection and self-knowledge.

The flat horizons around Aigues-Mortes with their fever-laden marshes are an invitation to *rêverie* and omnipotent expansion of the Self, but the tower in its age-old solidity is fixed and immobile at the centre of this vast panorama. It is tense and con-

---

ment to Pascal. Mercanton calls Pascal Barrès' "supreme intercessor" (p. 211), but he observes that it is through his sensibility and not through his intelligence that he acceded to the sense of mystery in Pascal's works. He concludes: "La poésie de Barrès, faute de religion, n'est pas une vraie poésie religieuse. Elle est une poésie de la religion, une interprétation poétique du problème religieux, une musique, à la fois intime et vague, sur les émotions et les rêveries qui, pour une âme d'homme inquiet et de poète, se dégage du mystère des choses" (p. 217).

[14] Jean-Pierre Richard has analyzed the same duality in the works of Stendhal and Baudelaire ("Connaissance et tendresse de Stendhal" and "Profondeur de Baudelaire"). Of Baudelaire he writes: "Point de vie, certes, sans expansion: mais la logique de l'expansion étant de finalement briser la vie, il lui faudra soit freiner l'épanchement vital, soit l'équilibrer par d'autres mouvements intérieurs qui joueront au contraire dans le sens d'un resserrement et d'une avarice d'être" ("Profondeur de Baudelaire," in *Poésie et profondeur*, Éditions du Seuil, 1955, p. 133).

tracted upon itself, a symbol of continuity in change, of an eternal past projected into an eternal present:

> J'atteignais la plate-forme de la tour, et mon cœur se dilata à voir l'univers si vaste. Le passage de cette tour qui m'oppressait à cet illimité panorama de nature exprimait exactement le contraste de l'ardeur resserrée d'un saint Louis et de mes désirs infiniment dispersés (JB p. 67).

Philippe has established an analogy between his own cult and Saint Louis, whose spirit has been in turn assimilated to the tower, so that both express the same conflict. He sees in Saint Louis' struggle to impose a unity in his soul through submission to religious faith an analogy with his own quest for a "formula to which he could conform" (p. 67). Saint Louis and the tower represent the possibility of self-discipline, the constraining of all his disparate impulses around one central point.

The same drama is embodied in the contrast between the austere and immobile Castillian sierras, of which Toledo and the Escurial are the expression, and the plain of Andalucia in Southern Spain. Chapter II of *Un Amateur d'âmes* is entitled "Les Jets alternés d'Espagne," and its subject is this confrontation of asceticism and emotional expansion. The Escurial is "the translation in granite of Castillian discipline" (SVM p. 48). The arid rigidity of the North is opposed to the softness, to the enchantment of Andalucia:

> Au nord, les Espagnes sont sécheresse: fécondes, abondantes quand même, leur aridité étant faite de sensibilité contractée. Au midi, c'est un fleuve irrésistible de sensualités (p. 47).

The opposition now is between fecund self-containment and a kind of sensual debauchery in which the Self is borne away uncontrollably (this idea is expressed, as often in Barrès' writing, by the image of the river).

In the dialogue between the chapel and the plain which concludes *La Colline inspirée,* the chapel is a "house of solidity" (p. 339), and again, a "stone of solidity" (p. 340), while the plain represents a source of *rêveries,* a primitive and anarchic mystical impulse:

> 'Je suis, dit la prairie, l'esprit de la terre et des ancêtres les plus lointaines, la liberté, l'inspiration.'
> El la chapelle répond:
> 'Je suis la règle, l'autorité, le lien; je suis un corps de pensées fixes et la cité ordonnée des âmes.' (p. 339).

The opposition is between discipline, fixity, and order on the one hand, and liberty and daemonic inspiration on the other. However, an apparent contradiction can be observed here, for the inspirational source of mystical exaltation is the hill on which the chapel is situated. Indeed the chapel becomes the focal point of the hill in this concluding dialogue. Similarly, the spiritual and physical elevation of the *tour Constance,* of Toledo, and the Escurial is at the origin of Philippe's and Delrio's ecstatic meditations, while at the same time they represent a principle of solidity. In the same way, eternity is equally discernible beneath the surface of the plains. The barren landscape around Aigues-Mortes denotes the same permanence as the tower. The terrace of Delrio's garden overlooking the Castillian *mesa* is described in these terms: "le plus doux et le plus âpre des balcons sur un pays noble et désert comme la mer, mais immobile autant qu'un cimetière" (SVM p. 38). The Toledan landscape can evoke the instability of the sea, but its immobility speaks of changeless death.

In fact, these *hauts lieux* function as multiple symbols, containing in themselves the essential drama of which they are the center. They serve to inspire, but they are also manifestations of the concentration and discipline which are necessary to counter the dangers of inspiration. And always they represent a permanence beyond the endless succession of brief moments passing into death. Looking out over the plain, Philippe comes to the painful awareness that he is just "a minute of this land" and that "for that instant it dwells in him" (JB p. 68), but the tower arouses a feeling of eternity. The expansion of the plain is the expression of Life which cannot be possessed in its mortal immediacy. On the other hand, the tower which signifies the possibility of self-possession, is the very image of Death in its rigid immobility. The only permanence is in death, so the only refuge from the indefinitely repeated death of the ephemeral present is in the permanent solidity of Death itself.

Images of death are always closely associated with these privileged places. In *Un Amateur d'âmes,* he writes of Toledo's "character of eternity" and the impression it gives of being out of time (p. 34). When Delrio and La Pia visit Toledo at night, "a sepulchral moon adds to the silence of death" and the walls of the monasteries are "funereal" (p. 67). The inscription *Hic jacet pulvis, cinis et nihil* in the cathedral seems to reveal the "great secret truth." The Escurial with its "eternal blue granite" is a "fearsome vault" in the midst of the sierras (p. 50). Aigues-Mortes is twice described as a tomb: "Aigues-Mortes ... est toujours à son poste, étendu sur la plaine, comme un chevalier, les armes à la main, est figé en pierre sur son tombeau" (JB p. 47). The death like stillness of the old city is clearly contrasted to the fleeting manifestations of the present:

> Ce lieu, qui se présente naturellement sous un aspect d'éternité, met en un clair relief combien est furtive la grâce de Bérénice, combien fugitive chacune de mes émotions les plus chères. Aigues-Mortes est une pierre tombale, un granit inusable qui ne laisse songer qu'à la mort perpétuelle (p. 84).

The harsh light of death, like the cold brilliance of a Mediterranean winter sunset throws into "clear relief" the transience of the emotions which inhabit him. The result is a kind of framing or isolation of the emotion in a sharply intensified lucidity. The awareness of death, like the sense of loss or impossibility, heightens both emotion and consciousness. In fact, for Barrès, the analytic process is inseparable from the pain of death.

Ruins, churches, and cemeteries come to symbolize for Barrès the essential duration through history of the land upon which they are built. Aigues-Mortes and Toledo are both described as ruins, and he calls the *tour Constance* "the true memory of the land" (JB p. 65). Cemeteries speak of the same fidelity to the past which is so important for him. And of course, they are the key with which he is able to unlock the emotional reserves of Lorraine. The monotonous plains of his native province with its humble villages and highly cultivated land could not produce the dramatic emotion of deathlike sterility he found in the landscapes of the South, but its cemeteries, its historical sites, and the feeling of an age-old human tradition imprinted upon the land led him to the same meditation upon death and continuity, for it is quite literally composed of the spiritual presence of his dead ancestors.

Already in *Un Homme libre*, Barrès had formulated what is the essence of his doctrine of "the land and the dead," as he meditates on the land of Lorraine:

> Là, chaque pierre façonnée, les noms même des lieux et la physionomie laissée aux paysans par des efforts séculaires nous aideront à suivre le développement de la nation qui nous a transmis son esprit. En faisant sonner les dalles de ces églises où les vieux gisants sont mes pères, je réveille des morts dans ma conscience (pp. 95-96).

His doctrine of the dead, his ancestor worship, and his reconstruction of Lorraine according to his personal vision are clearly related to his meditations on death in the more "romantic" landscapes. Much of his work can be seen as a reflection upon the immortality of the mortal — his struggle with an anguished awareness of death at the heart of every civilization, of every individual life, and even of every passing moment.[15]

In spite of the practical applications of his cult as a means of political regeneration and personal therapy, Barrès' Lorraine is an abstract and tragic meditation. He turned to his homeland in search of a principle of permanence, but by his own avowal, the civilization and culture of Lorraine were dead (*Un Homme libre*, pp. 119-122, "La Mort de Lorraine"). Perhaps this was an essential condition for his emotional possession of his province — just as Venice, Aigues-Mortes, and Toledo are also presented as dead. They are only the petrified memory of their past glory. At best, he found in the idea of the collective soul a kind of immortality beyond the brief span of individual life. The feeling that his soul

---

[15] Joseph Barbier, discussing the theme of the dead in *La Colline inspirée*, writes: "C'est pour lutter contre la mort elle-même qu'il va solliciter le secours des morts en assurant la profonde continuité de son être. Toutes ses démarches restent ainsi imprégnées de son égotisme originel" (*Les Sources de La Colline inspirée de Maurice Barrès*, Nancy, Berger-Lavrault, 1957, p. 36).

was composed of elements that had survived from thousands of his dead ancestors and that it would itself survive in those that followed him is a consolation and a refuge (HL p. 181). The dissolution of even his most ecstatic emotions seemed less irrevocable. But it was a relative immortality, still situated within time. Barrès finds in the wider life of the race a permanence beyond the life of the individual similar to that which Malraux finds in Art and Culture.

The only thing which is beyond the law of death is the vital energy of the universe. Each of its phenomenal manifestations may perish, but "the soul of the universe" is indestructible. On the same page as the comparison of Aigues-Mortes to a tombstone, we read: "Je touchais avec une certitude prodigieuse la puissance infinie, l'indomptable énergie de l'âme de l'univers que jamais le froid ne prend au cœur, qui ne se décourage sous la pierre d'aucun tombeau et qui chaque jour ressuscite" (JB pp. 84-85). Death is the mode of transformation of this force as it strives infinitely to create the future. From the point of view of this creation, the death of each successive present is no longer an irrevocable loss, but a necessary preparation for the future in which it is assumed, perpetuated, and surpassed. This is the basis of Barrès' doctrinal belief in the people and in nationalism. The loss of each present as it recedes into the past can only be meaningful if the future continues that past, if the transformation of the world can be seen as necessary and determined. The destruction of each unique individual and of each unique moment that he lives is less catastrophically final when his existence can be situated along the chain of a wider collective existence. Unable to create a meaningful present, Barrès attaches himself to the past and tries to justify present and future in terms of that past. Memory and the visible monuments of dead presents are signs which point the way to the future.

But in fact these signs tell him very little of the future; they speak only of their own melancholy abandonment. This rather desolate vitalism is an attempt to give a certain dynamism to what is essentially a static vision [16] and also to derive a principle of

---

[16] Gide accused Barrès of being indifferent to the future and to any real idea of progress (*Journal. 1889-1939*, Gallimard, "Bibliothèque de la Pléiade," 1951, pp. 1064-65).

energy from a basically morbid temperament. For a political doctrine to be effective, it must propose a means of creating something in the future; yet we can see that the effectiveness of his nationalism is singularly limited by the fact that it is the consecration of the death of the past. The intervention of Barrès' analysis freezes the present moment; it introduces a rupture and an ending, it is a kind of entombment. The beauty of his "universe" is rigid and immobile, fixed in the clear light of detached meditation. In spite of his insistence upon continuity and the vital impulse towards the future, the position which he adopts with regard to all that he observes is always that of the man who comes *afterwards* to contemplate the ruins. His inclination carries him towards that which has been lost or which has failed, and his meditations set the seal of esthetic immobility upon that loss and that failure.

It is significant, too, that his nationalism should be grounded in the notion of an unconscious principle of growth. The death of the Ideal in the 19th Century entailed the end of the upward striving of the Romantics. Consciousness was turned downwards, towards the Unconscious, towards Instinct, which could perhaps become a new Unknown. Barrès' tendency to reduce the awareness of the sublime to its origins in physiological categories is symptomatic of the new turn of the human mind seeking to explain man by the lowest common denominator — his underlying instincts. Emotion, cut off from its roots in a higher moral sphere, turns to this new underlying substratum to ensure its unity in time. The Unconscious, of which renewed desire is the permanent expression, assures the unity in succession which is his essential doctrine. From it emerges the whole complex of notions such as evolutionary becoming, growth, the garden, and ultimately nationalism and the myth of Lorraine. The cult of the Self leads to an exaltation of growth as a value it itself, independent of its finality. The organic sense of growth, participating in an unconscious cosmic movement, is an escape from the obsession with death, and his nationalism is thus the glorification of an organic process of becoming.

Moreover, his nationalism is less a political theory than a private cult held up for the emulation and admiration of his disciples. His political "ideas" are essentially subjects of meditation, indeed of prayer. Barrès invites his readers to join him in a series of "spiritual exercises" designed to bring an upsurge of emotion (nostalgia, regret, pity, reverence, mystical exaltation) to bear on the idea of the land of France. Religious emotion and nationalism converge in his doctrine of the land and of the dead. His cult of the national past permits him on the one hand to indulge in the melancholy mysticism of death and annihilation, and on the other to assert a human solidarity in his relations with other men, while consoling himself with the intellectual comfort of a limited theory of the transmigration of souls. His cult is a means of harnessing mysticism to his doctrine of limited immortality.

Nostalgia is the only creative force for Barrès, for only regret can confer fullness and value upon the world. Loss and death are necessary to deliver up the world for complete emotional possession,[17] and the cult of emotion becomes the cult of death. The nostalgic strives to convert the energy of that regret into a system for dealing with time. Bérénice is the allegory of this attempt. She represents the soul of the universe striving to develop into the future, and she is Philippe's guide to an instinctual grasp of life, but regret is her mode of being. Her instinctual fidelity is to the lessons of the past, and the memory of her dead lover is the source of all her energy. Thus, in this novel of multiple analogies reflecting one upon the other, Bérénice too must die before Philippe can truly possess her and assimilate the lesson she embodies. Just as the tower is a sign of permanence by virtue of the image of Death that it evokes, so the eternal quality of Bérénice, underneath that "furtive grace" of her living Self, can only be possessed after her Death. Then only can she be resurrected in her moral essence (the title of Chapter XIII is "Petite-Secousse n'est pas morte!").

---

[17] There is a curious example of Barrès' tendency to view the present as if it were already the past in the preamble to the first number of *Les Taches d'encre:* "Et peut-être qu'après avoir été un agréable entretien cet hiver avec des amis bienveillants, elle [la gazette] me sera plus tard un aimable souvenir, la brochure un peu fanée que je relirai en souriant, tandis que la sœur infirmière, avec onction, me tendra la douce tisane au bon poète devenu mûr" (p. 388).

Sensuality, the immediate and spontaneous response to the world, is perhaps the guide to authentic understanding, but its lesson can only be known and possessed in the past. Meditation, which begins as the sensation dies, is the tomb in which the past can be resurrected. Solitude, itself a kind of death, is the condition in which the world arises anew, *sub specie aeternitatis*,[18] and ordered according to the harmony of thought. The "hauts lieux," dramatizing the presence of eternity at the center of infinite dispersion, represent the fixity of thought and meditation in the endless flow of present sensation. As the chapel says in the passage to which I have already referred: "Je suis un corps de pensées fixes" (*La Colline inspirée*, p. 339). From the heights of egotistical isolation, the Self organizes the world according to its idea. Like the tower of Aigues-Mortes, the Self is an immobile central point of which the tomb is the image.

The death of Bérénice releases Philippe from the immersion in the present, and all the fragmentary sensations which were concentrated around her can yield their emotional essence. In memory, she becomes the point of crystallization around which the moral analogies fall into place in a harmonious whole. Bérénice and the landscape, reduced to idea, cease to exist in the confused indefiniteness of time and take on their ideal beauty. The death of Bérénice can be seen as an allegory of the novel itself, for her passing is the passing of present beauty which, seized in memory and meditation, is recreated in the moral coherence of the analogical "universe." Her death symbolizes the process of moral assimilation of the physical world which Barrès first announced in his meditation upon Venice in *Un Homme libre* and which constitutes the basic technique of *Le Jardin de Bérénice*.

The garden is Barrès' greatest image for the universe in which egotism is rendered fruitful by acceptance of the natural principle of growth.[19] In *Un homme libre,* Philippe explains that his method

---

[18] "Que chacun se construise son univers avec ses moyens! rentrons dans notre domaine, qui n'est pas le pire; il nous appartient de juger les choses *sub specie aeternitatis*" (JB, p. 122).
[19] Thought about man and his society in the 19th century was dominated by the analogy with the natural sciences. Images of harmonious growth were very common in literature, as well as in historical and scientific writing. Barrès shared this organic view of life, and perhaps

is to train his emotions to give the finest possible blooms (p. 183). However, his soul is at first incapable of sturdy production: "Je suis un jardin où fleurissent des émotions sitôt déracinées" (JB p. 76). Because of the extreme artificiality of his cult, his emotions have no strong roots in the soil of authenticity. He must learn through Bérénice to submit to the "creative energy, the sap of the world" (p. 126). "Un arbre, sans rien soupçonner des belles théories de l'École forestière, sait mieux qu'aucun garde général quand il doit se développer, dans quel sens, selon quelle forme. C'est le secret de la vie que trouve spontanément la foule" (JB p. 144). Thus the lesson of Bérénice is a counter to the sterile self-affirmation which was the conclusion of *Un Homme libre,* when Philippe refused to develop his instincts ("Que mes vertus naturelles soient en moi un jardin fermé, une terre inculte" [p. 237]).

The ideal is a selective development of the natural force within him, in which conscious manipulation is allied to instinctive acceptance. Philippe's method is to combine the unreflecting virtues of Bérénice with the rational approach of Charles Martin, the engineer. In the last resort, the tree cannot be left to grow entirely according to its instinct. The garden, then, is the place in which some natural features of the outside world will be admitted, but its anarchic growth will be excluded. It is the image of a selective, personal recreation of reality in which the Self can most efficiently develop. Already in *Sous l'œil des barbares,* this was the cynical advice of M. X... as he sketched a vision of the young man's "universe": "C'est un verger où vous n'avez qu'à vous satisfaire, ingénument, par mille gymnastiques" (p. 180). But Philippe's garden has to be more than a paradise of self-indulgence. It must facilitate the creative fulfillment of the Self and it must be morally instructive.

The garden is an image of a reconstructed "universe" in which the cultivation of the Self is possible, but it is also an enclosed space, a refuge in which the individual is hidden from the gaze of the Barbarians. "Le premier soin de celui qui veut vivre, c'est de s'entourer de hautes murailles; mais dans son jardin fermé il introduit ceux que guident des façons de sentir et des intérêts

---

the influence of Taine is preponderant in this. See "L'Arbre de M. Taine" in *Les Déracinés.*

analogues aux siens" (HL p. 101). The notion of closure is essential in Barrès' universe. His thought, his writing, and his meditations are a personal haven, impregnable and perfect in its exclusion of outer chaos. *Un Homme libre* was composed under the urgency of this desire for sencurity [20] in a methodical structure of his own making. In the midst of the vulgar precipitation of the everyday life that he was forced to live, Barrès staked out a domain of fertile calm in which his inner Self could develop at its ease. The *arrière-boutique* of Montaigne's more confident egotism has become the splendid garden of Barrès' inner retreat, "L'égotisme est une propriété close" (JB p. 177), Philippe exclaims; "Une propriété close, c'est vrai! mais où nous nous cultivons et jouissons" (p. 178).

The garden is the ordered inner space of the mind, carefully circumscribed by the protective walls around. Within the walls, at the heart of the rigid sterility of analysis and immobile self-contemplation, is fertile ground arranged systematically for the best esthetic and utilitarian effect. In a sense, the garden is an image of the beauty of Barrès' writing, for it is within the limits of his books that his meditations bear their fruit. The garden, the artificial "universe," is the symbol of the esthetic and moral recreation of reality which he achieves in his meditations upon landscapes, art, history, and literature.

Thus the "universe" is the abstract domain in which the outside world is reduced to intelligible moral signs. Its fecundity is guaranteed by the convergence of sensuality and moral abstraction. By the outward movement of projection, the Self materializes its sensations in allegories and in the mirror of analogy. Bérénice,

---

[20] Bernhard Baur discusses Barrès' profound sense of insecurity, his lack of confidence in himself, and he, too sees the garden as a symbol of refuge: "Der Ausdruck *Jardin fermé* kommt öfters vor, auch im J. d. B. Die *tour d'ivoire* des Barrès scheint eigentlich weniger abgelegen im Traumlande zu liegen, wie bei den Romantikern, als vielmehr umlagert von 'Barbaren'" (*Inhalt, Motive, Stil*, p. 105).

He analyzes Barrès' various attempts to escape towards a refuge in which he would be unassailable: evasion into dreaming, into dandyism, into forgetfulness, into irony, and into what is fixed and solid. He interprets the fortified town of Aigues-Mortes as a symbol of his desire to take refuge in a systematic approach to life — as, for example, his doctrine of the land and the dead.

Marina, and La Pia incarnate his sentimentality and his sensual longing, while art, landscapes, history and literature again reflect the categories of his own soul. On the other hand, the real world is rendered abstract. It is dematerialized to permit a moral possession, an interiorization. The inner distance of the Self is concretized by the images which establish a geography of the soul, while the real landscape is reduced to ideas. It becomes in turn a literal image of the soul, a vast analogy reflecting the categories of the Self.

If the egotist projects himself outwards, it is to study his reflection and absorb it back enhanced. It allows him to contemplate his sensibility narcissistically, but it also permits him to separate it from himself, to analyze it, to possess it. The harmony Barrès seeks is that of an exchange between the Self and the outside world. The cultivation of the Self is harnessed to a creative moral and political stance in the world. But the Self will only accept the categories of the outside world, bend itself to a system or to an ideology, if the outside world will in turn conform to the categories of the Self.

The little garden around Bérénice's home, in its harmonious closure, becomes an analogy of the whole world reduced to its ideological unity. The clarity of the universe, the perfect relevance of each part to the whole, replaces the unmanageable phenomenal world. The Self, maintaining its analytical lucidity, no longer dissolves itself in the matter of its ecstatic contemplation. Each part, each fragment retains its separate identity, but the sterility of fragmented multiplicity is overcome by the *illumination* of the whole in a total emotional coherence. By analogy, each part of the universe reflects its separate clarity upon every other, and all illuminate the Self which is the active principle of their harmony. It is the analogy of painting that Barrès uses to illustrate this vision of harmony. As Philippe meditates upon the lessons of Tiepolo in Venice, he admires above all the luminosity of his works: "Où l'harmonie naît d'une incomparable vibration lumineuse. — Ainsi mon unité est faite de toute la clarté que je porte parmi tant de visions accumulées en moi" (HL p. 189). The sharp lines of separation which isolate objects are blurred so that they melt into each other, while still retaining their form and their distinctive color. They seem to penetrate each other, just as

Barrès' analogies break down the separateness of the various objects of his solitary meditations.

The absolute silence and the solitude of the tower are the image of his meditation in which nothing distracts his thought. The world is spread around him under his intellectual vantage point, and, as he meditates, the confusion of the whole begins to fall into shape. The "reflective" method of Charles Martin isolates the various parts and the "intuitive" sympathy of Bérénice binds them together in a living unity as the analogies emerge. The light of the setting sun illuminates the entire landscape, bringing out the relief with its declining rays and covering all forms with the same Mediterranean clarity. Barrès always preferred the moment of sunset when the sun makes every detail stand out sharp and clear in its perfect definition, while the intensity of the light seems to be even greater in spite of the approaching dark. The earth seems to glow with the accumulated light of the day, every object seems to be in itself a luminous source throwing back light into the sky. The diversity of the world is united in the splendor of this "luminous vibration." And then as the day draws to an end and the world prepares to slip into oblivion, the true meaning of the spectacle takes shape in his mind. In the beauty of the sunset, between day and night, the world seems lifted out of time, immobilized for a glorious instant before sliding into its nightly death. Between present reality and forgetfulness, the world assumes its greatest glory in memory, in the ideal reality of meditation from which the analogical "universe" rises up transformed and redeemed.

CONCLUSION

In their different ways, each of the three books which comprise the trilogy of *Le Culte du moi* is a dramatized *rêverie*. What Barrès means by his "universe" in these books is the consciousness of the world as a reality experienced in solitary meditation. These novels are the ordering and systematization of his inner dialogue during these meditations. They are the fruit of his withdrawal into the private world of the Inner Self, allegorical accounts of a mental experience beyond that of everyday life with its particular events, real people, and concrete problems. The themes of the trilogy are quite literally abstracted from the facts of Barrès' life: his spiritual awakening at school, his friendships as a young man, his life in Paris, his travels, his convalescence in Lorraine, his electoral compaign; but the novels are in no way a narrative account of these experiences. The events are transposed and refined until they lose all existential meaning.

Although the insistent use of the first person and the idea of literature as a cult of the Self make Barrès the most "self-centered" of authors, he never writes about himself in a personal way in his books. He reveals little about his private life in *Le Culte du moi*, nothing about his friendships (who is Simon?), nothing about his family, nothing about any specific relationship with another person, nothing about his everyday emotions, hopes, and frustrations. In this sense, Barrès is the least "human" of writers. The Self he reveals so immodestly is an abstract Self, always alone and standing above the ordinary man at that level of awareness for which problems and emotions are depersonalized. The psychology of his characters merges with collective sensibility and general attitudes to life. The young man in *Sous l'œil des barbares* and the character who says "I" in *Un Homme libre* have no name and no personality. It was only at the request of his readers that Barrès called his hero Philippe at the beginning of *Le Jardin de Bérénice*. There is desire in his books, but it is pure desire, and abstract psychological force underlying the Self's relations with the world. When love appears in his works, it is a vehicle for expressing some other theme. It never attains another person, but merely serves to crystallize certain forms of sensuality and sensibility. This is why, although Barrès is apparently so confiding, he is in reality so distant and so infinitely reserved.

He developed the habit of always writing from the vantage point of this abstract Self, and to judge from the solitary attitudes and exemplary poses that he struck, he tended to confuse his own existence with this self-created being within him. It is not difficult to see how he so easily became a collective idol, when he so strikingly generalized his own personality. De Gaulle, in his self-appointed historical action in France, carried this kind of depersonalization of the Self to its limit. Even those who knew the general quite well, always found the same sphinx-like public figure.

In Barrès' work, it is difficult to make a distinction between texts of a private nature and texts written as propaganda for his nationalism. He always relies on a demonstration of his "intimate" emotions in order to carry the conviction of his reader when he is talking about Lorraine or France. Since his doctrine is founded on these emotions experienced in solitary meditation, he must constantly lead his reader back to this central illumination. The intensity of his "private" emotion is the guarantee of the general "truth" that he is propounding.

His doctrine of authenticity required that he submit the individual self to the discipline of a collective national consciousness, so that his private meditations on his spiritual needs and on the way in which Lorraine nourished his soul acquired an immediate exemplary value for all his readers. His solitude was like that of the priest or monk whose withdrawal is for the sake of all the faithful and whose intimate prayers redound to the good of the public soul. Barrès meditating "his" truths in Lorraine was surrounded in spirit by the invisible presence of all France in search of its being. When he wrote "I," thousands read "We."

His writing is founded on the exposure of a certain interiority, so that sincerity is a major value in his work. In the early books, this sincerity has a truculent, disrespectful, assertive quality when self-exposure is used as a weapon *against* the world. Later on, when he uses the veracity of his emotions to ground his doctrine, it becomes a question of fidelity. It is the continual demonstration of the same unchanging being. But it is the intensity of this sincerity, of this faithfulness to his innermost Self, which justifies the work. Clearly the self-exposure in his works is quite different from the retrospective revelations of Rousseau. As we have seen, there is nothing privately personal in *Le Culte du moi:* there are no confessions, no justifications, no attempts to draw the reader into the secrets of motivation. His sincerity is of a generalized intellectual and abstract nature like everything else in his work.

Writing for Barrès is the concentration of discontinuous inner reflection into a dramatic meditation. Meditation is thus the principal mode of his imagination. Not only can his works be described as long meditations in themselves, but they often contain accounts of particular meditations which are the points of highest intensity in those books: Philippe on the *Tour Constance* in *Le Jardin de Bérénice*, Marina and André in Venice in *L'Ennemi des lois*, Philippe in Lorraine and Venice in *Un Homme libre*. At the heart of his work is the lyrical meditative essay. Most often, it is inspired by a place: Venice, Aigues-Mortes, Castille, Greece, Lorraine, any landscape or historical site that moved him. *Du sang, de la volupté et de la mort, Greco ou Le Secret de Tolède, Le Voyage de Sparte,* and *Amori et dolori sacrum,* those most typical of his "personal" works written after *Le Culte du moi,* are constructed in this way.

The lyrical meditation is also an important element in his naturalist and political novels. *Leurs Figures* ends in the gardens of Versailles where François Sturel retires to meditate the lessons of his defeat. The noble park seems to speak words of consolation and wisdom to him as he contemplates its stately harmony. The landscapes around Metz are as important as the characters in *Colette Baudoche*. Chapter Six in *Au service de l'Allemagne*, "La Pensée de Sainte-Odile" is a full scale lyrical and spiritual meditation upon the moral lessons contained in one of the "hauts lieux" of Alsace. And, of course, *La Colline inspirée,* the most mystically spiritual of any book Barrès wrote, arises out of his very special cult of Sion in Lorraine as a subject for meditation. These lyrical meditations are always high points of intensity in the books where they occur and they irradiate the whole text in as much as they resume all its themes and usually point to its deep meaning.

Much of his work, then, is organized around the carefully staged confrontations of his own emotions and his own consciousness with selected scenes of the outside world. These encounters of the Self and the World, constructed in the space of the literary text, generate an intensification of both lucid consciousness and lyrical emotion which are experienced as having an almost "metaphysical" value in that they permit an exalting sensation of self-possession and spiritual penetration. Sometimes they are transposed into the form of the allegorical novel as in the early works, sometimes they serve as the ideological and moral nucleus around which he constructs his political novels, and sometimes they are presented directly as in the travel books. The center of his work is the meditation upon a spiritually and morally significant place where he gathers around him the forces of his soul in fecund solitude. On the periphery are the innumerable essays and speeches of a propaganda nature which repeat and defend the original insights provided by these privileged moments.

Taking *Le Culte du moi* as a whole, one can see that Barrès is striving to integrate three kinds of material. First of all, there is the introspection and self-analysis which is the subject of the trilogy. The other material is organized around this account of his search for self-possession and self-embellishment. Secondly there is the expression of his sensibility. All this works are marked by passages of great intensity in which feelings of melancholy and regret, elation and desire, are inserted into the text. There is a lyrical rhythm to his writing; his prose is punctuated by frequent poetic passages and there is usually a rising curve of intensity in each of his books, culminating in a high point, a chapter or a section of highly charged emotion: the visit to Venice in *Un Homme libre,* the death of Bérénice, the death of La Pia in *Un Amateur d'âmes.*

The third element is the broad category of Barrès' reflections upon the world around him: descriptions of places to which he travelled, of towns, museums, historical sites, and landscapes; biographical and historical essays; criticism of literature and art; and the exposition of his psychological, philosophical, and political ideas. This is what one might call essay material and it constitutes a large part of his literary production. Clearly the formula of *Le Culte du moi* was very effective in enabling him to integrate his talents as journalist, satirist, critic, travel writer, and even on occasion as historian, into his higher ambition to be a novelist. In *Un Homme libre,* for example, he has brought together material widely different in nature and origin. The section on the intercessors is really literary criticism, the passages on Lorraine contain a historical essay, and Philippe's journey to Venice makes use of his own travel notes in that city. It is the way in which all the elements are related to the Self and the search for a moral truth common to them all that constitutes the unity of this book.

A glance at the table of contents of *L'Ennemi des lois* is also very revealing. The novel is manifestly a collage of political, social, and biographical essays loosely integrated into the allegorical story of Marina and André Maltère. Even his naturalist novels are constructed from essay material. The action is continually slowed, sometimes stopped for whole chapters, while he introduces pages of analysis and speculation. In *Les Déracinés,* for instance, there are three successive chapters which are little more than transposed essays. "L'Arbre de M. Taine" presents his reflections upon Taine's ideas in the form of a dialogue between Taine and Roemerspacher and then between Roemerspacher and his friends. The next chapter, "Au tombeau de Napoléon" is a meditation upon the national hero, again dramatized in the form of a dialogue among the group of friends. "La France dissociée et décérébrée" is quite simply a political analysis of the ills from which the country was suffering, introduced directly by Barrès.

The texts develop from the basic meditative experiences as elaborations of groups of related themes. The difference in the kind of text depends on the mode of elaboration and the overall context. For example, the account of Philippe's visit to Italy in *Un Homme libre* is different from the account of Barrès' visit to Toledo in *Greco* only to the extent that it is integrated into the hero's fictional quest for self-knowledge. The meditation on the *Tour Constance* at Aigues-Mortes in *Le Jardin de Bérénice* organizes the raw material of Barrès' impressions into both the thematic continuity of the novel as a whole and the allegorical fiction centered around Bérénice. However, any temptation that the reader might have to assert that the fictional dimension adds nothing essential to the text is quickly dissipated if he compares a chapter of Greco with one of the texts from *Le Culte du moi*. There is a tension, an urgency, and a rhythm in the earlier texts which are quite lacking in the direct account of his meditation. The transposition which occurs in the passage from Barrès to Philippe changes the tone completely. The fictional first person of the trilogy is quite different from the voice of Barrès, the traveller and collector of emotions. The maudlin sentimentality, the self-centeredness, and the rhetorical inflation which irritate so many of today's readers make their appearance only when what was original in *Le Culte du moi* degenerates into mere procedure in his later writing.

This form of composition by the articulation of a group of themes around an object of contemplation (landscape, work of art, personage, historical event) gives a non-linear structure to his books. In the case of *Le Jardin de Bérénice* and *La Colline inspirée*, the entire text is organized around the inspirational value of a single place: Aigues-Mortes and Sion. But his works often have several such focal points, so that the text tends to be grouped around a number of centers. Barrès proceeds by a progressive widening of the thematic network away from the center, outwards in concentric circles as it were. The most characteristic feature of his literary imagination is this constructive activity around a central object. In his best works, he succeeds admirably in imparting a dynamic quality to this process which permits him to transcend the immobility inherent in meditation. It is not the movement of plot or description which creates this dynamism, but the dialectical organization of the themes themselves.

It is for this reason that Barrès' achievement cannot be judged entirely by the yardstick of the "finished work." The unity of his work resides in the totality of his writing, because each individual book is a part of that one continuous "text" which he elaborated throughout his life. And I have tried to show that this text *is* his life, in the sense that Barrès confused life and literature and that he used literature as a means of self-creation. The individual books are different modes of the basic text generated by his ongoing confrontation with the world. Thus his most characteristic creations are those lyrical meditations, the work of a moralist and a poet, which are the point of departure and the nuclei of almost all his books.

Although Barrès was not in close contact with the Symbolist group, his notion of literary value was strongly marked by the current of taste which ran all through the eighties and nineties and which produced the Symbolist esthetic. Among his books at school, he developed a precocious sense of spiritual value and a haughty contempt for all that is base and morally inelegant. By early choice he saw himself as a literary aristocrat at odds with the modern world. In the name of an idealism which insists that we cannot know reality anyway, since we project our own temperament onto things, he rejected the literature of description and observation. He prized suggestivity, inwardness, nobility of mind, high spirituality, and stylistic elegance.

So to some extent *Le Culte du moi* can be considered a Symbolist work. It is concerned with the inner life of a single character who is none other than the author's fictional self; it refuses to give any value to the outside world other than that which the individual projects upon it; and it makes considerable use of allegory and non-realistic evocation to represent mental realities. A comparison with a novel like *Sixtine* (subtitled *Roman de la vie cérébrale*), which Remy de Gourmont published in 1890, reveals a striking convergence of themes: the sense of solitude and pessimism; the subjective idealism; the assertion that the Self is the only reality; the attempt to cultivate a harmonious world within the mind; the idea that the loved one is the creation of the imaginative faculties; the monastic tendency; the religious atmosphere which envelops the novels; the use of religious psychology as a model in the attempt to control one's psychic mechanism.

It can be argued, then, that Barrès is in many ways a product of the Symbolist epoch. But, although the themes and the esthetic orientation of his works, as well as the elitist character of his revolt, bear the stamp of the eighties, it is not really possible to classify even his early works as Symbolist or Decadent. In the first place, his revolt is quite different in the direction it takes.

It is not a Baudelairian artistic revolt, but rather an attempt to rediscover the essential person under the cultural layers accumulated in an overrefined civilization. Barrès is trying to break out of the cerebrality and solipsism which were de-energizing the cultural elite of the country. His hero, Philippe, unlike so many Symbolist heroes, is not an artist and he does not seek esoteric avenues of escape. He does not attempt to shut himself off from the outside world in the perfected universe of his imagination. He does not refuse life or accept in advance the impossibility of living. It is true that *Le Culte du moi* begins by denying the reality of the world and by declaring that the self-created ego is the only refuge, but this is the first, negative, stage in a dialectic designed to re-establish contact with the world.

Where Symbolism turns away from the world in pursuit of esthetics, Barrès turns back to it in the search for an ethic of involvement. In spite of the fact that he downgrades action and gives a primacy to thought and inner attitude, the main thrust of the trilogy is back towards the world in which he seeks a formula for active living and community. The "free man" is not just the one who is in perfect control of his own psychic powers, but also the one who can dominate and use the outside world for his own aggrandizement. There is an impulse in his works towards the world as something to be possessed and conquered. The frequency of his use of metaphors and expressions drawn from the vocabulary of militarism is an indication of the depth of this imperialism of the sensibility.

Le Jardin de Bérénice is a complex investigation of what is at one level a political question arising out of his involvement with the Boulangist movement. Barrès is asking himself what kind of action is most suited to help the popular masses evolve in accordance with their real needs and deepest inclinations. And, in general, his books do not exclude the world in spite of their allegorical closure and their roots in solitary meditation. He was a great traveller and he was immensely curious about the countries he visited. Germany, Italy, Spain, Greece, the Orient, and different regions of France provide the background and often the thematic material for his books. Although he came to cling to his national identity in an exclusive manner, he was a cosmopolitan figure in many ways. To some extent, he participated in the movement which was to open up the horizons of French literature after many years of stay-at-home writing. At a time when Symbolism was turning its back on life, the originality of Barrès resided in the way he raised the basic problems of existence. How can one belong to oneself in a world in which one is subject to so many pressures and sollicitations? How can one rediscover one's authentic being or attach oneself to spiritual values in an age of relativism? How can one live and act in the world? [1]

His success at the end of the century was due to the fact that he seemed to offer an alternative to the Symbolist-Decadent impasse, while retaining much of the estheticism, idealism, and refusal which were peculiar to this form of sensibility. But perhaps the most essential reason for his immense popularity was his ability to capture the spirit of adolescent revolt in his books. The first two novels of *Le Culte du moi* in particular are deeply rooted in the experience of the schoolboy and the very young man in his first contact with the adult world outside school: they take seriously the anxieties of late adolescence. It was to the young that he addressed himself in *Sous l'œil des barbares* and *Un Homme libre* — the latter is even dedicated to the students in the *lycées* throughout the country. *Le Culte du moi* was written for a generation of *bacheliers* whose elitist sentiment it flattered and whose problems it so accurately reflected. He seized their imagination by a passionate diagnosis of what they recognized as their own malaise.

His exaltation of solitude and his arrogant affirmation of the Self as the only reality in an uncertain and oppressive world were very much an adolescent reaction to the problem of growing up. The trilogy seemed to clear the board of all the old problems and to encourage every young person to make a fresh start for himself. His symbolic jettisoning of the old *maîtres à penser* in *Sous l'œil des barbares* seemed to mark the beginning of a more hopeful era, an escape from the deadening feeling of pessimism and sterility which was stifling intellectual circles. These two

---

[1] Michel Raimond underlines the importance of this shift in emphasis which Barrès gives to the novel: "Le 'qui suis-je' et le 'comment vivre?' l'emportaient sur la peinture des mœurs" (*La Crise du roman*, p. 75).

early novels held out the hope that spiritual energy could once again be accumulated in the mind and expanded in the world. Particularly exciting for the young was the way in which they are organized as a quest for a key to unlock one's own hidden treasures, and, by extension, to unlock the treasures of the world. *Un Homme libre* is the story of a search for power — for power over oneself and over the world.

In these years when it was fashionable for young men to express their dissatisfaction with the world in the form of fastidious individualism, his public responded instinctively to this cult of the Self. The subtle elegance of his style was very attractive to a generation for whom revolt had to be esthetically distinguished. And there was a combination of lyrical passion, nervous delicacy, and lucid, calculating intellectuality in his works that appealed to an age which was at once hypersensitive and extremely cerebral.

Barrès helped to open up a new perspective for the novel by exploring a different relationship between the writer and his world. He placed the Self at the center of the novel and he took as his subject the nature of the Self's engagement in the world outside. He contributed to the tendency of the 20th century novel to be in itself a means of engaging the writer in the world. The novel becomes an extension of the writer's life or inversely his life is an extension of the novel. *Le Jardin de Bérénice* rises out of a reflection upon the nature of political action and the conclusions of the novel point beyond it to Barrès' doctrine of nationalism. For Montherlant and Malraux, both profoundly influenced by Barrès, the novel is a means of completing their own lives or examining their actions in the world. Taken a step further, the novel becomes a means of questioning the "metaphysical" basis of life. Malraux, Camus, and Bernanos extend their personal quest to universal allegory.

The writer no longer sees his role as that of fable maker or, at the other extreme, teller of the world. His writing creates neither an imaginary world nor a historical reflection of the real world, but a more real world in which he, as an individual, finds himself and defines himself. Literature has moved closer to life in that it begins to see itself as an action in the world. Thus the writer is often not just discovering and defining for himself alone, but for other men. He becomes something of a moral guide, even a prophet, engaged in the world, and suggesting ways of feeling it and acting in it. Barrès was one of the first of those "princes of youth" of which the 20th Century has seen so many. Barrès, Gide, Malraux, and Camus were more than just successful writers; their works and their lives became rallying points for successive generations of young people. They were purveyors of attitudes for living. Their work assumes a resonance, a direct opening upon life itself which goes far beyond mere literature. For the man of the 20th Century, literature indeed became an ideological garden reflecting the world in terms of his will and desire for action in it.

Barrès' decision to write about himself and his stance in the world could thus resolve both his literary dilemma and his intellectual anguish. By choosing his own life as his subject, he sought to break down the antinomy between dream and action, between literature and life, which had paralyzed the 19th Century. However, he was never quite successful in this enterprise. He fell somewhere between the two, never truly effective as a political figure and never quite able to produce a great literary creation. He was disowned and denied by the succeeding generation in a way that Gide, Montherlant, and Malraux, although their moment has passed, have never been denied. The very vehemence of the attack against him was the measure of the hopes he had raised and then failed to fulfill. He failed to create a myth, and success in the 20th Century was to depend on the novelist's ability to create an imaginary world which invites its readers to extend its meaning into their own lives.

But *Le Culte du moi* did not lead to any true creation within literature. *Un Homme libre* provided a method and an affirmation of the Self which was seized upon by other writers for their own creations. However, *Le Jardin de Bérénice* was only the image of a creation. It was a splendid metaphor for Barrès' doctrine and the way he intended to view the world. It did not have that kind of open-endedness which would allow its meaning to expand and reverberate in the mind of the reader. It pointed too absolutely to one meaning which was too narrow to inspire either his readers or Barrès himself. The garden was too closed upon itself, its atmosphere too stuffy. This atmosphere of stuffiness and oppressive constraint is increasingly preponderant in his later work as he became a victim of his own manner and prisoner of his doctrine.

Le Jardin de Bérénice is truly a "closed garden" in that its symbolic meaning on one level refers to the technical procedure by which it was created. On the other hand, the novel is incomplete in as much as the actual content of the garden, its meaning, must be sought outside the text, in Barrès' private drama and in his political conviction. The creation which *Un Homme libre* announced and of which *Le Jardin de Bérénice* is the image is fulfilled not in literature but in life. *Le Culte du moi*, in spite of its atmosphere of closure to the outside world, its elaborate thematic coherence, and its studied removal from everyday contingencies, is not a creation based upon life, but an essay about attitudes to life. Barrès was writing novels about how to recreate the world, but they send him back into the arena of lived reality in which recreation is impossible. Unlike Stendhal or Baudelaire who resolve very similar conflicts in their literary creations, in imagination rendered permanent by words, Barrès creates no ideal life in which to fulfill his "Universe." His reconstruction of the world is not an end in itself, but a lesson which refers him endlessly back to the real world for its application. His evocations of Venice, Aigues-Mortes, and Spain convey the emotions one should feel and they elaborate a method for seeing the beauty of these places, but they do not completely realize that ideal beauty in themselves. In spite of all Barrès' efforts, his books remain ultimately sterile, because they seem to be the scaffolding of a work which was never constructed. Perhaps, for him, the exaltation of writing was such that he strove above all to render that exaltation, without conveying its substance. These works are always *about* exaltation, *about* emotion, *about* creation, *about* harmony, but they are never quite these things themselves.

Yet *Le Jardin de Bérénice* remains Barrès' most successful work, I believe, for it provides the most accomplished example of his technique and a metaphor of it. The ideological garden is an image of his reconstruction of the real world into a harmonious totality through meditation in which art, history, literary allusion, and landscape are merged with his personal experience and sensibility. The death of Bérénice which concludes the narrative becomes the symbol of the act of writing by which immediate experience is converted into the permanent emotion of remembered beauty.

It is in his books that Barrès strove to create this ideal "universe" in which the Self and the world are merged and embellished. But it is at this point that we can observe a tension between two principal axes of his work. On the one hand, the dynamics of Barresian egotism (by which I understand a consciously constructed attitude designed to resolve the problems of the individual's involvement in the real world) point to something positive and active. *Le Culte du moi* proposes a method for breaking out of the sterility of nihilism and for redeploying spiritual energy in the world. Beyond the trilogy, his doctrine of nationalism proposes a similar program of action and involvement. On the other hand, the very act of writing creates a paradox, because as a writer Barrès sees literature as the fulfillment of the world. As artistic constructions his books become an end in themselves. His "universe" is a static construction, turned in on itself as the mirror of his own self-contemplation. His works stand poised between Narcissicism and Ideology just as the writer himself stands between Literature and Life, perhaps never quite able to reconcile the two.

BIBLIOGRAPHY

For a complete bibliography of works by Barrès and of books and articles about him until 1948, consult Alphonse Zarach, *Bibliographie barrésienne. 1881-1948*, Paris, Presses universitaires de France, 1951.

Since 1920, Barrès' works have been published in separate volumes by the Librairie Plon. Plon has also completed an edition of his collected works, annotated by Philippe Barrès, in the 20 volumes of *L'Œuvre de Maurice Barrès* in the collection "Au club de l'Honnête Homme," 1965-68.

ALSO AVAILABLE IN PLON EDITIONS:

Mes Cahiers. Textes choisis par Guy Dupré. Préface de Philippe Barrès. Paris, Plon, 1963.
Chronique de la Grande Guerre, 1914-1920. Introduction et choix de Guy Dupré. Commentaire de Philippe Barrès. Paris, Plon, 1968.
Maurice Barrès and Charles Maurras. *La République ou le roi. Correspondance inédite (1888-1923).* Paris, Plon, 1970.
Several titles are currently available in the Livre de poche edition: *Le Culte du moi, Les Déracinés, Colette Baudoche, La Colline inspirée, Un Jardin sur l'Oronte, Leurs Figures.*

SELECTED BIBLIOGRAPHY:

Aragon, Louis. "En guise de préface." Vol. II of *L'Œuvre de Maurice Barrès.* Paris, Plon, Au club de l'Honnête Homme, 1965.
Baillot, A. *Influence de la philosophie de Schopenhauer en France.* Paris, Vrin, 1927.
Bancquart, Marie-Claire. *Les Écrivains et l'histoire. D'après Maurice Barrès, Léon Bloy, Anatole France, Charles Péguy.* Paris, Nizet, 1966.
Barbier, Joseph. *Les Sources de La Colline inspirée de Maurice Barrès.* Nancy, Berger-Levrault, 1957.
———. Critical edition of *La Colline inspirée.* Nancy, Berger-Levrault, 1962.
Baudelaire, Charles. *Œuvres complètes.* Paris, Gallimard, Bibliothèque de la Pléiade, 1961.
Baur, Bernhard, *Versuch über Inhalt, Motive, Stil in Le Culte du moi von Maurice Barrès.* Strasburg, Heitz, 1937.

Bernanos, Georges. *Les Grands Cimetières sous la lune*. Paris, Plon, 1938.
Beucler, A. "Visites à Barrès." *Revue des deux mondes* (May-June 1956).
Blanche, J.-E. *Mes Modèles*. Paris, Stock, 1928.
Blanc-Peridier, A. *La Route ascendante de Maurice Barrès*. Paris, 1925.
Boisdeffre, Pierre de. *Barrès parmi nous*. Paris, Amiot-Dumont, 1952. 2nd ed., enl., Paris, Plon, 1969.
———. "La Jeunesse de Maurice Barrès." *Revue des deux mondes*, August 15, 1962, pp. 569-580.
Borie, Jean. *Le Tyran timide*. Paris, Klincksieck, 1973.
Borreli, G. "Barrès et la psychologie de l'art." In *Actes du colloque*, Nancy, 1963.
Bourget, Paul. *Essais de psychologie contemporaine*. Paris, Lemerre, 1883.
———. *Le Disciple*. Édition définitive. Paris, Plon, 1901.
Bradley-Looke, B. *Quelques traits baudelairiens chez Barrès*. Thesis, Strasbourg, 1962.
Bréhier, Émile. *Histoire de la philosophie*. Tome II. *La Philosophie moderne*. Fascicule No. 4. *Le XIXe siècle après 1850. Le XXe siècle*. 5th ed., rev. Paris, Presses universitaires de France, 1968.
Brogan, D. W. *The Development of Modern France*. London, Hamish Hamilton, 1940.
Brombert, Victor. *The Intellectual Hero. Studies in the French Novel. 1880-1955*. Philadelphia and New York, J. B. Lippincott, 1961.
Brunetière, Ferdinand. "Après une visite au Vatican ou La Science et la religion." *Revue des deux mondes*, 127 (January 1, 1895).
Cabanis, Georges. *Rapports du physique et du moral de l'homme*. Vol. I of *Œuvres philosophiques*, Paris, Presses universitaires de France, 1956.
———. *Degré de certitude de la médecine*. Vol. I of *Œuvres philosophiques*, Paris, Presses universitaires de France, 1956.
Caplain, J. *Maurice Barrès, ami des jeunes*. Paris, H. Goulet, 1924.
Caramaschi, Enzo. "Egotismo e storia in Barrès." In *Études de littérature française*. Paris, Nizet, 1967, pp. 295-353.
———. "Maurice Barrès et Venise." In *Études de littérature française*. Paris, Nizet, 1967, pp. 255-291.
Carassus, Émilien. *Barrès et sa fortune littéraire*. Bordeaux, Guy Ducros, Collection: Tels qu'en eux-mêmes, 1970.
———. "Les Débuts parisiens de Maurice Barrès." *Revue d'histoire littéraire de la France*, No. 2, 1965.
———. "Premières ironies de Maurice Barrès à l'égard de Renan." *Annales publiées par la Faculté des lettres de Toulouse. Littératures*, 12 (November 1965), 33-37.
———. "Le 'départ inquiet' de Maurice Barrès. Note sur la genèse de *Sous l'œil des barbares* (chapitre 1er)." *Annales publiées par la Faculté des lettres de Toulouse. Littératures*, 14 (September 1967).
———. "Maurice Barrès feuilletoniste." *Revue d'histoire littéraire de la France*, 70, No. 1 (January-February 1970), 90-97.
Castex, Pierre-Georges. "Aux sources d'*Un Homme libre*." *Revue d'histoire littéraire de la France*, 59 (January-March 1959), pp. 71-86.
Charpentier, Th. "Barrès et l'art lorrain de son temps." In *Actes du colloque*, Nancy, 1963.
Clouard, Henri. *La "Cocarde" de Barrès*. Paris, Nouvelle Librairie Nationale, 1910.

Clouard, Henri. *Histoire de la littérature française du Symbolisme à nos jours.* Paris, Albin Michel, 1947.
Cocteau, Jean. *La Noce massacrée.* Paris, A la Sirène, 1921.
──────. *Le Rappel à l'ordre.* Paris, Stock, 1926.
Curtis, Michael. *Three against the Third Republic. Sorel, Barrès and Maurras.* Princeton, Princeton University Press, 1959.
Curtius, Ernest Robert. *Maurice Barrès und die geistigen Grundlagen des französischen Nationalismus.* 2nd ed. Hildesheim, Georg Olms, 1962.
Davanture, Maurice. "Barrès, Burdeau et Bouteiller." *Actes du colloque,* Nancy, 1963.
Dietz, J. *Maurice Barrès.* Paris, Renaissance du livre, 1927.
Domenach, Jean-Marie. *Barrès par lui-même.* Paris, Seuil, Écrivains de toujours, 1954.
Doty, Charles Stewart. "Maurice Barrès and the fate of Boulangism: the political career of Maurice Barrès, 1888-1906." *Dissertation Abstracts,* XXV, no. 11 (May 1965), 6564-6565. Ohio State diss.
Dubois, Jacques. *Les Romanciers français de l'instantané.* Bruxelles, Palais des Académies, 1963.
Dufay, Pierre. "Maurice Barrès au quartier Latin." *Mercure de France,* 169 (1924), 92-99.
Duhourcau, François. *La Voix intérieure de Maurice Barrès d'après ses cahiers,* Paris, Grasset 1929.
Duvignaud, Jean. "Barrès l'étranger." *Nouvelle revue française,* 171 (March 1 1967), 491-497.
Empaytaz, Frédéric. *Reconnaissance à Barrès.* Paris, Les Presses françaises, 1925.
Evans, Silvan. *The Life and Work of Maurice Barrès. A short centenary study.* Ilfracombe, Stockwell, 1962.
Faure-Biguet, J.-N. *Maurice Barrès, son œuvre.* Paris, 1924.
Fernández, Ramón. *Barrès.* Éditions du Livre Moderne, 1943.
Frandon, Ida-Marie. *L'Orient de Maurice Barrès. Étude de genèse.* Geneva, Droz and Lille, Giard, 1952.
──────. "Connaissance de Barrès." *L'Information littéraire,* 1958
Frohock, W. M. "Trauma and Recoil: The Intellectuals." *The Massachusetts Review,* 12, no. 3 (Summer 1971), 528-533.
Frye, Northrop. *The Anatomy of Criticism: Four Essays.* Princeton, Princeton University Press, 1957.
Gaxotte, P. "Barrès et l'enracinement." *La Table ronde* (April 1957).
Gide, André. *Feuillets d'automne.* Mercure de France, 1949.
──────. *Journal. 1889-1939.* Paris, Gallimard, Bibliothèque de la Pléiade, 1951.
──────. *Romans, récits et soties. Œuvres lyriques.* Paris, Gallimard, Bibliothèque de la Pléiade, 1958.
Giraud, Victor. *Les Maîtres de l'heure. Maurice Barrès.* Paris, Hachette, 1922.
Godfrin, Jean. *Barrès mystique.* Neuchâtel, A la Baconnière, 1950.
Goosse, Marie-Thérèse. "A propos de *Sous l'œil des barbares.*" *Revue d'histore littéraire de la France,* 66 (1966).
──────. "Maurice Barrès et Barbey d'Aurevilly." *Les Lettres Romanes,* 22, no. 4 (November 1 1968), 353-370.
Gouhier, Henri. *Notre Ami Maurice Barrès,* Paris, Éditions Montaigne, 1928.

Gouhier, Henri. "Pascal et Barrès." In *Actes du colloque*, Nancy, 1963.
Gourmont, Rémy de. *Le Livre des masques*, Paris, Mercure de France, 1896.
———. *Sixtine, roman de la vie cérébrale*, Paris, Mercure de France, 1921.
Grover, M. "The Inheritors of Maurice Barrès." *Modern Language Review*, 64, no. 3 (July 1969), 529-545.
Hughes, H. Stuart. *Consciousness and Society. The Reorientation of European Social Thought 1890-1930*. New York, Alfred A. Knopf, 1958.
Huret, Jules. *Enquêtes sur l'évolution littéraire*. Paris, Charpentier, 1891.
Jourda, Pierre. "La Venise de Maurice Barrès." *Venezia nelle letterature moderne*, No. 11 (1962), 192-201.
King, Sylvia M. *Maurice Barrès. La Pensée allemande et le problème du Rhin*, Librairie ancienne Honoré Champion, 1933.
Lalou, René. *Maurice Barrès*. Paris, Hachette, 1950.
Laurent, Marcel. "Pascal et Barrès." *L'Auvergne Littéraire, Artistique et Historique*, No. 187 (1965), 1-21.
Lehmann, A. G. *The Symbolist Aesthetic in France, 1885-1895*. 2nd ed. Oxford, Blackwell, 1968.
Levaillant, J. "Barrès et la rêverie." In *Actes du colloque*, Nancy, 1963.
McShine, J. Orville, *Maurice Barrès, journaliste* Port-au-Prince. Haiti, Presses nationales d'Haiti, 1966.
Madaule, Jacques. *Le Nationalisme de Barrès*. Paris, Le Sagittaire, 1942.
Massis, Henri. *Barrès et nous*. Paris, Plon, 1962.
Mauriac, Pierre. "La position religieuse de Maurice Barrès." *Actes de l'Académie Nationale des Sciences, Belles Lettres et Arts de Bordeaux*, 1962, pp. 19-28.
Maurice Barrès. Actes du colloque organisé par la Faculté des lettres et des sciences humaines de l'Université de Nancy (Nancy, 22-25 oct. 1962). Ouvrage publié avec le concours du Centre national de la recherche scientifique. Nancy, 1963.
Mercanton, Jacques. *Poésie et religion dans l'œuvre de Maurice Barrès*. Lausanne, F. Rouge et Cie., 1940.
Miéville, Henri L. *La Pensée de Maurice Barrès*. Paris, Éditions de la Nouvelle revue critique, 1934.
Mondor, Henri. *Maurice Barrès avant le Quartier Latin*. Paris, Ventadour, 1956.
———. "Premières lectures de Barrès." *Revue de Paris* (January 1, 1956).
Moreau, Pierre. *Maurice Barrès*. Paris, Le Sagittaire, 1946.
———. *Ames et thèmes romantiques*. Paris, Corti, 1965.
———. *Barrès*. Paris, Desclée de Brouwer, "Les écrivains devant Dieu," 1970.
———. "Autour du culte du moi; essai sur les origines de l'égotisme français." *Archives des lettres modernes*, No. 7 (December 1957).
———. "Maurice Barrès ou l'homme libre." In *Actes du colloque*, Nancy, 1963.
Mourey, G. "Maurice Barrès critique d'art." *Revue bleue* (September 2 1911).
Mourot, J. "Barrès et Chateaubriand." *Actes du colloque*, Nancy, 1963.
Naïs, Hélène. "Le Bestiaire de Barrès." In *Actes du colloque*, Nancy, 1963.
O'Brien, Justin. *The Novel of Adolescence in France. The study of a literary theme*. New York, Columbia University Press, 1937.

Ouston, P. A. "Landscape in Barrès' art of persuasion." *Forum for Modern Language Studies*, 6, no. 4 (October 1970), 355-367.
———. *The Imagination of Maurice Barrès*. Toronto and Buffalo, University of Toronto Press, 1974.
Petitbon, P.-H. *Taine, Renan et Barrès. Étude d'influence*. Paris, Les Belles Lettres, 1934.
Picard, Michel. "La conscience tragique dans *Le Culte du moi* de Maurice Barrès." *Revue des sciences humaines*, n. s., 23, fasc. 128 (October-December 1967), 587-611.
Pilon, E. *Maurice Barrès*. Paris, Maison du livre, 1926.
Raimond, Michel. *La Crise du roman des lendemains du naturalisme aux années vingt*. Paris, Corti, 1967.
Renan, Ernest. *Œuvres complètes*. 10 volumes. Paris, Calmann-Lévy, 1947-1961.
Ricardou, Jean. "Expression et fonctionnement." *Tel Quel*, Vol. 24 (Winter, 1966).
Richane, Loutfi. *Barrès et l'Espagne*. Dactylographié. Thèse 3e cycle. Paris, 1968.
Richard, Jean-Pierre. "Connaissance et tendresse chez Stendhal." In *Littérature et sensation*. Paris, Seuil, 1954.
———. "Profondeur de Baudelaire." In *Poésie et profondeur*. Paris, Seuil, 1955.
Richard, Noël. *A l'aube du symbolisme*. Paris, Nizet, 1961.
———. *Le Mouvement décadent*. Paris, Nizet, 1968.
Rops, Daniel. "Barrès, Venise et le goût de la décadence." *Abeilles et pensées* (January-February 1929).
Ruff, Marcel. "Barrès et Baudelaire." *Hommage au doyen Gros*. Gap, 1959.
Situation de Maurice Barrès. *La Nef*, No. 33 (August, 1947).
Soucy, Robert. "Barrès and Fascism." *French Historical Studies*, 5, no. 1 (Spring 1967), 67-97.
———. *Fascism in France; the Case of Maurice Barrès*. Berkeley, University of California Press, 1972.
Soury, Jules. *Histoire des doctrines de psychologie physiologique contemporaines. Les fonctions du cerveau; doctrines de l'école de Strasbourg, doctrines de l'école italienne*. Paris, Bureaux du "Progrès Médical", 1891.
Sternhell, Z. *Maurice Barrès et le nationalisme français*. Paris, Armand Colin, 1972.
Swart, Koenraad. *The Sense of Decadence in Nineteenth Century France*. International Archives of the History of Ideas. The Hague, Martinus Nijhoff, 1964.
Taine, Hippolyte. *De l'intelligence*. 3rd ed. rev. and enl., 2 vols. Paris, Hachette, 1878.
———. *Voyage en Italie*. Paris, Hachette, 1910.
Taveneaux, René. "Barrès et la Lorraine." In *Actes du colloque*, Nancy, 1963.
Ternois, R. "Barrès et le Gréco." *Actes du IVe Congrès de littérature comparée*, Paris, 1961.
Tharaud, Jérôme and Jean. *Mes Années chez Barrès*. Paris, Plon, 1928.
Thibaudet, Albert. *La Vie de Maurice Barrès*. Vol. II of *Trente ans de vie française*. Paris, Gallimard, 1921.
———. "Barrès et Michelet." *Nouvelle Revue Française* (January 1 1929).

Tronquart, Georges. "Barrès et l'Université." In *Actes du colloque,* Nancy, 1963.
Uitti, K. D. *The Concept of Self in the Symbolist Novel.* 'S - Gravenhage, Mouton, 1961.
Valéry, Paul. *Poésies, Mélange. Variété.* Vol. I of *Œuvres.* Paris, Gallimard, Bibliothèque de la Pléiade, 1957.
Vallet. "Maurice Barrès critique d'art." *Revue bleue* (August 4 1934).
Vettard, Camille. "Maurice Barrès et Jules Soury." *Mercure de France,* No. 170 (March 15 1924), 685-95.
Vier, Jacques. "Barrès et le culte du moi." *Archives des lettres modernes,* Nos. 10-11 (March-April 1958).
———. "Ernest Renan personnage de Maurice Barrès." *Annales de Bretagne,* 71 (1964), 423-428.

The Department of Romance Studies Digital Arts and Collaboration Lab at the University of North Carolina at Chapel Hill is proud to support the digitization of the North Carolina Studies in the Romance Languages and Literatures series.

www.ingramcontent.com/pod-product-compliance
Lightning Source LLC
Chambersburg PA
CBHW020417230426
43663CB00007BA/1208